SHOOTING TIMES

GUIDE TO ACCURACY

SHOOTING TIMES
GUIDE TO ACCURACY

HOW TO BE A TOP SHOT WITH RIFLE, SHOTGUN, OR HANDGUN

EDITORS OF *SHOOTING TIMES*

INTRODUCTION BY JOEL HUTCHCROFT

Skyhorse Publishing

Skyhorse Publishing books may be purchased in bulk at special discounts for sales promotion, corporate gifts, fundraising, or educational purposes. Special editions can also be created to specifications. For details, contact the Special Sales Department, Skyhorse Publishing, 307 West 36th Street, 11th Floor, New York, NY 10018 or info@skyhorsepublishing.com.

Skyhorse® and Skyhorse Publishing® are registered trademarks of Skyhorse Publishing, Inc.®, a Delaware corporation.

Visit our website at www.skyhorsepublishing.com.

10 9 8 7 6 5 4 3 2

Library of Congress Cataloging-in-Publication Data is available on file.

Cover design by Tom Lau

Print ISBN: 978-1-5107-2077-0
Ebook ISBN: 978-1-5107-2080-0

Printed in China

TABLE OF CONTENTS

PART IV: OTHER FIREARMS

INTRODUCTION

The ability to strike a target with the utmost accuracy has been the objective of shooters ever since firearms were invented. During hunting, competitive shooting, informal plinking, or life-and-death situations, serious shooters have sought to shoot as accurately as they possibly can. The key, of course, is to become a better-skilled marksman. Equipment is important, too. Understanding what makes a firearm—let's say a centerfire bolt-action sniper rifle—more accurate is one step in the quest to be a better marksman. The same applies to handguns, shotguns, rimfire firearms, and even airguns. The *Shooting Times Guide to Accuracy: How to Be a Top Shot with Rifle, Shotgun, or Handgun* aims to help readers understand all these aspects and more.

Contained within these pages is the compilation of more than twenty articles that have been published in *Shooting Times* magazine and its special editions. These articles were specifically chosen because they target what we think is the most important information a shooter needs to know to better understand the art of accuracy. We believe that reading them—and applying their wisdom—will help you become a better shooter.

Some of the articles are equipment-specific, such as Layne Simpson's piece on what makes aftermarket rifle barrels accurate, Richard Mann's article on the most important part of a rifle, and Reid Coffield's step-by-step procedure for lapping an old rifle's barrel to improve its accuracy potential. Other chapters focus on shooting technique, such as Mann's commonsense approach to better marksmanship, Jeff Hoffman's report on how to master the invisible influence that wind has on accuracy, and J. Guthrie's treatise on scope techniques for long-range shooting.

In addition, Greg Rodriguez explains why tactical rifles are so accurate, and David Fortier tells you all about long-range military accuracy. Charles Petty demonstrates how a new barrel can improve your Model 1911 pistol's accuracy, and Tom Gaylord details how shooting airguns can improve your shooting skills. Also, Rodriguez and Terry Wieland offer shotgun shooting tips, Simpson provides his tips to improving muzzleloader accuracy, and Fortier shows you how to master the positions of NRA High Power competition.

All chapters were written by expert shooters and hunters who also are the most respected writers in the shooting industry with decades of experience to back up their opinions.

All in all, if you have an interest in the skills and equipment necessary to shoot one-hole groups, this book is for you.

Joel J. Hutchcroft
Editor in Chief, *Shooting Times*

PART I
TIPS FOR ACCURACY

By J. Guthrie

THE ART OF ACCURACY

Like any art, and riflemaking is an art, a tremendous amount of work and craftsmanship go into building a precision rifle. Here is an explanation of the process and the approach one custom house takes to produce supremely accurate rifles

CORBON 175gr
SIERRA MATCH
100 YARDS
.138"

S hortly after the first bullet was propelled toward a target by gunpowder, it is a near certainty the man behind the trigger was thinking of ways to make future shots more accurate. The quest to precisely place bullets at long range has absolutely consumed rifle builders and shooters. Whether the plans were penned with a quill and shaped with a file or drawn up with zeros and ones and executed by a robot, proficiency and accuracy are what define riflemen and rifles. Time has not changed that fact, but technology has made the end result more attainable.

There is not much in the way of hard data to confirm my suspicions of an increase in the number of guys offering up custom work and precision rifles, but it seems, even with my limited perspective in terms of years behind the trigger, that every day someone else hangs out his shingle and declares his rifles the best. With such a proliferation of custom houses, a whole new language has emerged—trued, blueprinted, coated, lapped, and bedded—and we are all quick to toss around the terms. But what do they really mean and is everyone comparing apples to apples? What goes into making a precision rifle?

I was fortunate to meet a gentleman a few years ago that struck me as just the guy to explain the process in detail. Jered Joplin at American Precision Arms has quietly built a stellar reputation for accurate rifles over the past 10 years. Collectively, the guys in his small shop have 45 years of riflemaking experience. APA makes a small line of aftermarket parts and builds everything from benchrest rifles to hunting rifles to rifles for SWAT teams. They handle every step of the process except machining the action from bar stock and putting rifling in the barrel. I liked Joplin's approach, especially after suffering through diatribes from numerous blowhards that proclaim their way is the only way and their rifles are the best, period. Joplin was quick to say there are plenty of great riflemakers, and his processes are time and range proven

but certainly not the only way to get the job done.

I spent a day last fall at Joplin's Jefferson, Georgia, shop and looked at all the different tools and techniques that go into building a precision rifle. Joplin first explained that while there are all kinds of rifles, heavy and light, large caliber and small, the principles that go into building an accurate rifle are pretty much the same. APA's craftsmen start with the action.

The Action

All actions are not created equal since rack-grade units could never hope to equal the precision or consistency of a custom action from companies such as Nesika or BAT Machine. They also do not cost more than a grand.

Regardless of where it comes from, each action gets a thorough inspection by APA's craftsmen, who carefully measure critical dimensions. The process is commonly called truing or blueprinting. Blueprinting, in its truest form, would involve matching every critical measurement to a set of drawings, which no one does. Truing simply assures that all the angles are square or perpendicular to one another and other parts are perfectly concentric. While used interchangeably, the two terms really mean different things.

"We measure every component to make sure it's perfect," Joplin said. "There are no guarantees, and nothing is taken for granted, since we've seen 'custom actions' that were out of square. Nesika and BAT have proven phenomenal over the years—their actions are right."

Every surface of a trued bolt and receiver will be parallel or perpendicular to the receiver's centerline.

A depth micrometer is used to measure from the receiver face to the boltface to determine headspace after truing. In addition to checking consistency, the measurements will also determine how the barrel is machined.

The rear contact surface of this bolt lug has been lapped into the lug seats. With both lugs lapped, the cartridge does not move when the rifle fires, and the bullet enters the throat perfectly straight.

I have seen truing and blueprinting offered as a service for the princely sum of $75. Should you encounter the same "gunsmith" or "custom rifle builder," run like hell since no reputable outfit could afford to do a proper job for that much money. Some guys call whacking off the receiver face square to the action body truing when the operation is really much more involved. The operation, depending on how out-of-spec the action is before the work begins, usually takes around two to three hours.

Joplin walked me through the steps using the most common action on which custom rifles are built—no surprise here—the Remington Model 700. Since the action is round and the bolt is round and there are no strange cuts for bolt stops, extractors, or leaf springs to power an extractor, getting things true is fairly simple. Every measurement starts from the action's centerline, and there are lots of ways to find the centerline.

"On a Remington 700, the receiver face is cut perpendicular to the action's centerline," Joplin said. "Then the barrel threads and lug seats are cleaned up and the bolt lugs are lapped into the receiver. The boltface is also cut square to the receiver face. We are trying to get everything either perpendicular or parallel to one another to within a few ten-thousandths (.0001) of an inch. That is the goal."

How does Joplin arrive at what to cut where? He does it through very careful and continuous measurements throughout the process. A professional-grade set of mea-

Joplin measures bolt nose recesses for length and width to make sure the bolt gets at least 0.10 inch clearance and does not touch the barrel at any point.

While APA has a proprietary set-up process, many riflemakers set up their lathes like this to machine a rifle barrel.

A live center finds the bore's centerline for precise, concentric machine work. The barrel's outside diameter should never be used as a starting point.

suring tools on the workbench is the first clue your riflemaker has a clue.

"We measure from the receiver face down to the lug seats from multiple locations, from 6 to 12 o'clock and then at 3 and 9 o'clock, to make sure things are square," Joplin said. "After the bolt lugs are lapped, which is the last step, we measure from the receiver face to the boltface to make sure they are consistent."

When metal must be removed, it has to be done very carefully and in the smallest of increments. An extra thousandth here or there could scrap an action.

"We are not hogging out huge amounts of metal here," Joplin said. "This operation has little or no effect on the way the bolt locks up inside the receiver and certainly doesn't reduce any inherent strength."

The goal is to get the bullet headed into the barrel as straight as possible and make the entire rifle ring like a tuning fork when powder starts to burn. Since it all starts in the action, it is critical that the action is perfect. The vibration, or more importantly the consistency of the vibration, that travels up and down the rifle when fired has a huge impact on accuracy.

"It all boils down to harmonics," Joplin said. "If there is a stress point or bad spot when the rifle is assembled, you will get inconsistent harmonics and a decrease in accuracy. Assuming the bullet is running at the right speed and at the right twist rate, the action should provide a harmonically stable platform so that the bolt does not torque and the barrel isn't canting. Lug contact is a great example. If one lug has more contact than the other, it can cause the bolt to cant towards the weak side when the rifle fires. That would torque the cartridge and send a bullet into the rifling off square."

The Barrel

It would be easy to devote an entire magazine to the art of barrelmaking. Heck, if every magazine in a year were devoted to the subject, the surface would barely be scratched. It is a black art that has driven men mad, and Joplin prefers to buy rifled and contoured blanks from established companies and preserve his sanity. While some custom houses do produce their own barrels, they are usually barrelmakers first and rifle builders second. The business is just that crazy.

The first step of the two- to three-hour operation is to turn down and thread the breech area. Cuts for the bolt nose recesses follow—no part of the bolt should touch the barrel. The chamber is then cut and checked for headspacing. Finally, Joplin cuts the crown and/or threads the muzzle for a brake or suppressor. The first step to successful barrel machining is indexing the lathe against the bore's centerline, not the outside diameter.

"You absolutely have to machine the barrel in a manner that lines up on the bore's true center, never on the outside diameter, otherwise the hole would not be perfectly concentric with the outside of the barrel," Joplin said. "Also, we want our chambers to only have a few ten-thousandths of runout."

Once threaded and chambered, the barrel can be mated with a

The bedding process creates a precise reverse of the action's footprint to relieve any firing stresses. An aluminum pillar is set into the stock at the same time and prevents the action screws from pinching or crushing the stock.

trued action. Torque ratings vary widely throughout the industry. APA likes 100 foot-pounds of torque, a slight crush fit, on hunting and tactical rifles. A benchrest shooter that switches barrels after just a couple thousand rounds might specify just 40 foot-pounds. The joining of barrel and action, obviously, is a critical operation.

"There is a fit and feel to the process," Joplin said. "You know what good threads feel like when assembling the parts. And you can't learn this from a book; it takes years. You have to be more than a lathe monkey; it's a craft."

The Stock

It is pretty obvious that to shoot accurately, you must address or hold the stock correctly. The same goes for the way the stock addresses the action and how it handles the recoil generated by firing. The good news is that science has provided stockmakers with materials impervious to everything but unskilled rifle builders armed with milling machines and drill presses. Bedding an action takes around

three days—the busy work only takes an hour or so—since the bedding epoxies must completely harden before firing commences.

Joplin first checks that the barrel has the right clearance. Old-school guys used to bed the barrel along its entire length. Now most guys completely free-float the barrel up to the recoil lug to eliminate the chance that the stock might produce the slightest pressure or change vibrations. Joplin carefully removes a small amount of stock material around the entire action's length and recoil lug. Wet epoxy is put into the stock, and the barreled action, taped up or coated with a release agent, is dropped into the stock and tensioned into place. The excess epoxy is removed, and the rifle is set aside until the new footprint sets.

"A bedding job eliminates stress on the action," Joplin said. "It looks simple, but it's an easy way to mess up a rifle's accuracy potential. It has to be done correctly."

Joplin likes adding aluminum bedding pillars to the stock, though he is quick to say it is possible to build an accurate rifle without them. Machined in house from aluminum stock, most measure 9/16 inch. F-Class rifles get 3/4-inch stainless-steel pillars. Radial and lateral grooves are machined into the pillar surface to prevent movement in the stock. The pillars are attached with the action screws and set into the epoxy at the same time as the action. Then the bottom metal is bedded to the stock. The two-part process takes more time but is more precise.

"We use aluminum pillars about 90 percent of the time to control the amount of torque applied by the action screws over a broad range of temperatures," Joplin said. "We also make sure the barrel and action are not canted at an upward or downward angle. There are not a lot of fancy measurements here; it's mostly eyeball work."

There is a simple layman's test to see if the stock is placing undue, accuracy-killing pressure on the action. First, stand the gun up on end with the recoil pad down on the ground. Place your index finger where the barrel and stock meet. Loosen the front action screw and see if the barrel moves. If it does, the action is stressed, and you might have accuracy problems as a result.

"You are looking to create a stress-free footprint of that action in the stock," Joplin said. "If there is something wrong in the stock or bedding, the gun will never reach its potential. Actually, quite a lot of work goes into making the stock right."

Quality Control

Besides the absolute care and precision with which parts are made and assembled, it is the quality-control checks at the end of the build process that separates a true custom rifle from rack-grade or production custom guns.

Throughout the build, individual parts are checked after machining and checked again for function with surrounding parts when assembled. The trigger—APA likes custom units from Huber Concepts, Jewel, and CG Jackson—is measured for consistency. Scope bases are carefully installed, and the rings are lapped.

"Our inspection is two pages long, single spaced, and nothing leaves here unless it goes through this check," Joplin said. "Like an airplane, the rifle doesn't leave the ground. It takes time, slows us down, and costs the customer more money, but it is what guarantees consistent accuracy, and that keeps the customer happy."

Rounds are fed through the action to check for feeding and extraction hiccups. Most factories function check their rifles with a few rounds and occasionally lot-test them for accuracy, but testing every rifle is usually out of the question. A production supervisor at a major manufacturer once told me that accuracy testing every rifle would add $75 to $100 to the retail price. APA has access to a private, 700-yard range and test-fires every complete rifle with match-grade ammunition from CorBon, Federal, and Black Hills.

"This is the crucial part of the process since our rifles are guaranteed to shoot half-MOA," Joplin said. "It's the only way we can ensure a rifle is 100 percent, and we want our customers to be satisfied in every way."

The Finish

The final step is putting a finish on the metal and stock if specified. A balance between cost, durability, ease of maintenance, and attractiveness must be struck, and the decision really depends on how

Joplin drops the finished action into a stock and secures it with 55 to 65 inch-pounds of torque.

the end user intends to apply the rifle. If there was the perfect coating, shooters would have found it years ago. APA does all its own finish work in-house using everything from Cerakote to standard mil-spec Parkerizing. Joplin's rifle builders have spent hours perfecting their mixtures and application techniques. Applying the finish usually only takes an hour or so, but cure times can run three or four days.

Delivering the Goods

Assuming all the parts were in-house and a guy had just one rifle to build, the entire process would take a couple of days, not counting drying time. So why does it take most custom houses five or six months to deliver a rifle?

Every complete rifle build is checked on a nearby range for accuracy. APA guarantees half-MOA with match-grade ammo.

Barrels are one of the biggest log jams. Most good barrelmakers stay months behind since near-perfect barrels simply cannot be rushed. Only a small percentage of custom rifle work can be accomplished without the barrel attached, so quite a few riflemakers have trays full of ready-to-go actions waiting on barrels. Stocks that match custom actions are often hand-built affairs, and most stockmakers set up their production runs in batches. So it can be several months before your favorite stockmaker gets around to making Surgeon- or Nesika- or BAT-compatible stocks.

A completed rifle can only be as good as the sum of its parts, so the higher quality components that go into the rifle, in theory, the more accurate it should be. That is true to a degree, but the way the rifle is assembled is the only way those components will ever realize their full potential. This is where the skills of the riflemaker come into play. Joplin was quick to say the occasional factory rifle will drive tacks, and less skilled riflemakers can turn out extremely accurate rifles. What moves a craftsman into the upper echelon is his ability to produce rifles that always shoot under any condition.

"The difference in a good gun and a great gun is in the small details," Joplin said. "When you guarantee your rifle to shoot half-MOA, every little part, every process, every machining step demands perfection."

It is Joplin's undivided attention throughout the process that demands the high prices paid for an American Precision Arms rifle. A few factory rifles will shoot as good as one of Joplin's rifles, but every gun wearing the APA logo, or the logo from any competent and conscientious riflemaker for that matter, will always shoot.

Hopefully this walk through a custom rifle build will give you a better idea of the terms used, the time it takes to build a precision instrument, and the exacting nature of the work.

Contact American Precision Arms at 706-367-8881 or online at americanprecisionarms.com.

What Makes Aftermarket

If you want to make one of your rifles capable of carving out tiny little groups by rebarreling it, here's everything you need to know about aftermarket rifle barrels.

BY LAYNE SIMPSON

A number of logical reasons exist for having an aftermarket barrel installed on a centerfire rifle. It could be that you're a varmint shooter and the barrel on your super accurate .223 or .22-250 finally gave up the ghost during your last prairie dog shootout. Or perhaps you have decided to transform the extra big-game rifle you never use into a heavy-barreled rifle capable of carving out tiny little groups. It could be that the caliber of a rifle you own really isn't what you need and you've decided on another chambering. Perhaps your heart is set on a chambering not available in a factory rifle. Then there is also the possibility that the only way the accuracy of a particular rifle can be improved is by upgrading it with a barrel of higher quality. Last but certainly not least, you may have decided to get into benchrest shooting in a serious way and realize that the only way to be competitive is to build a rifle capable of consistently keeping five bullets in the vital area of a housefly at 100 long paces.

Regardless of what your motive is, a number of questions will come up before you buy that new barrel. This report is offered to help you find the right answers.

How Much Accuracy Improvement You Can Expect

Contrary to popular opinion, the installation of an aftermarket barrel on a rifle doesn't automatically guarantee an improvement in its accuracy. Nor does it guarantee that the new barrel will even equal the original accuracy of the one it replaced. If a barrel is not installed by someone who knows what it takes to make a rifle shoot accurately or if the barrel

After rebarreling by Jarrett Rifles Inc., the sample .308 Win. Remington Model 700 VS's overall average accuracy improved by 54 percent.

After Rebarreling

Before Rebarreling

Rifle Barrels ACCURATE

is of poor quality to begin with, the rifle probably won't shoot any better than it did with its factory barrel. In fact, it might even shoot worse. On the other hand, if a good-quality barrel is installed properly, the increase in accuracy can be quite dramatic.

Two Remington Model 700 VS rifles I recently worked with are representative of how we all hope rebarrel jobs will turn out. Modified by Jarrett Rifles Inc., both rifles underwent the full accuracy enhancement treatment, which included trueing up the boltface, receiver ring face, and recoil lug bracket and lapping in the recoil lugs. Their trigger pulls were fine-tuned to a crisp two pounds, and relatively heavy barrels with muzzle diameters of .720 inch

were installed. The reason they fit so nicely into this story is due to the fact that I had an opportunity to accuracy-test both when they were brand-new and then sometime later when their factory barrels had been replaced by the aftermarket tubes.

As you can see in the accuracy comparison chart, the two rifles proved to be significantly more accurate after receiving the complete accuracy package, which is saying a lot since when both were new their factory barrels were quite accurate with some loads. In addition to improving overall accuracy by over 0.25 inch, the new .223 barrel also narrowed the accuracy spread between the various loads. When new, the factory barrel had ranged

from a best-load average of 0.478 inch to a worst of 0.891 inch for a spread of 0.430 inch. In comparison, the Jarrett barrel ranged from 0.311 inch to 0.610 inch for a 0.299-inch spread. Best-load accuracy improved by 34 percent while overall accuracy improved by 39 percent. The .308 reacted even better to its new barrel. Its best-load accuracy improved by 40 percent while its overall average improved by 54 percent. Like I said before, this is how we all hope a rebarrel job will turn out.

Stainless Versus Chrome-Moly

When a stainless-steel barrel and a barrel made of chrome-moly steel

The rebarreled .223 Remington Model 700 VS's overall accuracy improved 39 percent; its best-load average accuracy went from 0.478 to 0.311 inch at 100 yards.

are of equal quality their accuracy potential is the same. But stainless does have its advantages. In addition to its ability to resist rusting better than chrome-moly, it doesn't have to be blued or plated with a rust-resistant material. And since the stainless barrel is a bit more resistant to bore erosion, its accuracy life will be a bit longer. How much longer is influenced by a number of factors, many of which are within the control of the chap shooting the rifle, but most barrelmakers agree that when both are maintained the same, the stainless barrel will withstand the firing of from five to 10 percent more rounds.

I personally believe a stainless-steel barrel is worth its extra cost, especially when chambered for low expansion ratio cartridges. This type of barrel in .223 should go somewhere in the neighborhood of 6000 rounds before needing to be replaced, and it is not exactly uncommon to see some barrels last even longer. A stainless barrel chambered for a larger cartridge such as the .22-250 and .220 Swift should still be delivering long-range varmint accuracy at the 4000-round mark while a barrel chambered for one of the belted magnums, such as

the .240 Weatherby, .257 STW, .264 Winchester, 7mm STW, and .300 Weatherby, should still be delivering minute-of-whitetail accuracy at the 2500-round mark. When it comes to an even larger cartridge, such as

ACCURACY BEFORE & AFTER REBARRELING

Bullet	Powder (Type)	(Grs.)	Velocity (fps)	Accuracy (Inches) Before	After
.223 Remington Model 700 VS					
Hornady 50-gr. V-Max	VV N-133	26.0	3368	0.942	0.343
Nosler 50-gr. Ballistic Tip	W748	26.5	3319	0.754	0.382
Speer 50-gr. TNT	AA 2230	26.0	3407	0.733	0.412
Shilen 52-gr. HP	H335	26.0	3311	0.478	0.311
Sierra 53-gr. HP	AA 2495BR	26.0	3318	0.686	0.507
Sierra 53-gr. HP	Reloder 12	27.5	3379	0.855	0.480
Berger 55-gr. HP	H4895	26.0	3102	0.518	0.317
Nosler 55-gr. Ballistic Tip	IMR-4895	25.5	3240	0.781	0.358
Remington Premier 50-gr. SBT	Factory load		3318	0.717	0.519
Winchester Supreme 50-gr. Ballistic Silvertip	Factory load		3328	0.662	0.477
Black Hills 52-gr. HP/Moly	Factory load		3349	0.611	0.488
Hornady Varmint Ex. 55-gr. V-Max	Factory load		3266	0.891	0.522
Norma Diamond 55-gr. HP/Moly	Factory load		3274	0.692	0.610
Federal Gold Medal 69-gr. HPBT	Factory load		3019	0.721	0.412
Average Accuracy, Handloads				0.718	0.388
Average Accuracy, Factory Loads				0.715	0.504
Aggregate Accuracy, All Loads				0.717	0.438
.308 Remington Model 700VS					
Hornady 150-gr. SP	AA 2520	46.0	2865	1.399	0.712
Nosler 150-gr. Ballistic Tip	H4895	44.0	2862	1.323	0.522
Remington 150-gr. Bronze-Point	VV N-135	44.0	2822	1.501	0.896
Sierra 150-gr. SBT	W748	49.0	2871	1.106	0.597
Speer 165-gr. SBT	IMR-4895	45.0	2840	1.045	0.797
Hornady 168-gr. A-Max	AA 2460	42.0	2642	0.811	0.488
Sierra 168-gr. MatchKing	H335	44.0	2579	0.894	0.503
Nosler 180-gr. Ballistic Tip	Reloder 15	42.0	2755	1.214	0.517
Federal Hi-Energy 165-gr. Trophy-Bonded	Factory load		2884	1.724	1.210
Federal Gold Medal 168-gr. HPBT	Factory load		2662	1.645	0.602
PMC Match 168-gr. HPBT	Factory load		2702	1.119	0.723
Remington Match 168-gr. HPBT	Factory load		2655	0.955	0.542
Winchester Supreme Match 168-gr. HPBT	Factory load		2678	1.203	0.619
Winchester Supreme 180-gr. STBT	Factory load		2711	1.642	1.311
Average Accuracy, Handloads				1.161	0.629
Average Accuracy, Factory Loads				1.381	0.834
Aggregate Accuracy, All Loads				1.255	0.717

NOTES: The "Before" figures are for the Remington factory barrels. The "After" results are for Jarrett barrels. Accuracy is the average of three five-shot groups fired from a sandbag benchrest at 100 yards. Remington cases and Remington 7 1/2 primers were used in all .223 handloads. Winchester cases and Winchester WLR primers were used in all .308 handloads.

the .30-378 Weatherby, I believe a good barrel should still be accurate enough for big-game hunting at 2000 rounds. All of this assumes, of course, that a barrel is made of top-quality steel, it isn't heated up excessively by a lot of rapidfire shooting, and its bore is properly maintained.

Rifling Methods and Types

Several different methods are used to machine the rifling inside a barrel with the more common being button, cut, and hammer-forged. Remington, for example, hammer-forges its barrels while Savage uses the button method. Most of the smaller barrelmakers use the button-rifle process, but a few still use the cut method with Krieger being a good example. Lousy barrels can be made with either method. By the same token, as a

number of barrelmakers prove every day, either method can be used to make excellent barrels. The quality of a barrel is totally dependent on the quality of the steel used; the condition of the equipment used to drill, ream, and rifle it; and the skill of the fellow running the machinery.

I personally prefer button-rifled barrels, mainly because I have had such good luck with them through the years, but I am quick to admit that some of the best barrels in the world are rifled by other methods. Barrelmakers have also spent lots of time and money experimenting with various types of rifling, but when all has been said and done, conventional-form rifling with a uniform twist, just like you see in the typical factory rifle barrel, has won out every time. Just ask any world-class benchrest shooter.

Rifling Twist and Bullet Stability

I get lots of questions on rifling twist rates from readers, so here goes my answer to all of them. We all know that in order for a bullet to be stabilized in flight it must be rotated at an extremely high rate of spin. How fast it rotates is determined by two factors: the rifling twist rate of the barrel and how fast the bullet travels through the barrel. Rifling twist rates commonly run as slow as 1:66 inches for muzzleloaders to an extremely quick 1:7 inches when exceptionally long bullets are used in some centerfire rifle cartridges. And what do those numbers mean? A 1:66-inch twist simply means that the spiral-shaped rifling in the barrel rotates a bullet one time for each 66 inches of barrel the bullet travels

through. In other words, if a barrel with that rifling twist is 33 inches long, the bullet will be turned one-half revolution while it is traveling through the barrel. Moving to the opposite extreme, a bullet that travels through a barrel with a 1:7-inch twist will be completely rotated one time for each seven inches of barrel it travels through. If the rifled section of the barrel is 21 inches long, the bullet will rotate three times before it exits the muzzle.

The rotational speed of a bullet, or how fast it is spinning around its axis as it flies through the air, is determined by both its forward velocity and the rifling twist of the barrel. To calculate how fast a bullet is spinning in revolutions per second (rps) simply multiply its velocity times a constant of 12 and divide by the rifling twist rate of the barrel. As an example, when a bullet exits the muzzle of a 1:12-inch twist barrel at 2000 feet per second (fps) it is spinning at 2000 rps. An increase in either velocity or rifling twist rate will increase bullet rotation. Increase the velocity of that same bullet to 3000 fps, leaving rifling twist the same, and its rotational velocity will increase to 3000 rps. Reduce velocity back to the original 2000 fps but increase the rifling twist rate to 1:10 inches and the bullet will be spinning at 4000 rps. As you can see, a slight increase in rifling pitch rate increases the rotational speed of a bullet more than a considerable increase in velocity.

If a bullet is not rotated fast enough to be stabilized in flight, it will tumble through the air. When that happens its potential range is greatly decreased, and its accuracy goes to pot. The importance of this gyroscopic effect is easy to understand by anyone who attempts to throw a football as far and as accurately as possible. If the ball is allowed to tumble as it travels through the air, it won't travel very far and

.308 Rem. M700 VS

.223 Rem. M700 VS

A longer projectile requires a quicker rifling twist to stabilize it in flight.

is likely to veer off course and miss the target. But if the ball is thrown with one of its pointed ends aimed in the direction of flight and if a bit of spin is imparted to the ball as it leaves the hand, it will travel considerably farther and may even land exactly where the person throwing it wants it to go.

Something else to remember about bullet stability is this: The longer a projectile is in relation to its diameter, the faster it must be rotated in order to maintain a stable flight. Let's go back to the football, but this time I'll compare its flight characteristics with that of a soccer ball. Unlike the football that has to be rotated before it will become stable in flight, the round soccer ball can be thrown or kicked very accurately and for quite a long distance with little to no spin applied to it.

It works the same with the projectiles we commonly send flying through the air from firearms. This is why that extremely slow rifling twist rate of 1:66 inches I mentioned earlier is all we need for the barrel of a muzzleloading rifle that will be used only for the firing of round balls while a twist rate as fast as 1:7 inches might be required in order to stabilize an extremely long bullet of .22 caliber. Looking at it another way, I'll start with a .30-caliber spitzer boattail bullet

weighing 180 grains. If the weight of that bullet remains the same but its length is shortened by changing the shape of its nose from spitzer to round, it would not have to be rotated as rapidly in order to be stable in flight. If that same bullet were shortened even more by placing it in a powerful swaging die and squeezing it into a perfectly round ball, the rotational speed required in order to stabilize it in flight would be further reduced.

While choosing the correct rifling twist rate for a particular cartridge is important, some shooters have a tendency to make it a lot more complicated than it actually needs to be. They fuss, fret, and lose sleep at night trying to decide what twist rate to go with when making the right choice boils down to nothing more complex than telling the barrelmaker what cartridge the barrel will be chambered for and what bullets you intend to use, and then let him make the decision for you. If the gunsmith who will install

the barrel really knows his stuff, he is another source of the same information.

Another way to decide on rifling twist rate is to simply go with what is standard in the industry. A chart shown elsewhere in this report lists the standard twist rates for various cartridges as used by major barrelmakers such as Remington, Marlin, Winchester, Weatherby, Sako, and Savage. As you can see in the chart, rifling twists can vary slightly among the manufacturers, but they are close to the same for each cartridge.

For the benefit of those who really enjoy getting technical, I'll also mention the Greenhill formula, which was originally used to calculate the optimum rifling twist rate for lead bullets. A chap by the name of Sir Alfred Greenhill came up with it way back in the 1870s, but it works quite well today. To calculate the rifling twist rate needed for a particular bullet, divide 150 (constant) by the length of the bullet (in caliber) and then multiply by the diameter of the bullet (in inches). As an example, the diameter of Speer's 120-grain spitzer boattail is .257 inch and it is 1.125 inches long. Dividing that

Telling a competent gunsmith what chambering the aftermarket barrel will be chambered for is a good way to determine the barrel's correct rifling twist rate.

bullet's length by its diameter gives us a length in calibers of 4.38. Then by multiplying 4.38 times .257 we get a twist rate of 8.80 inches for that particular bullet. Rounding off to the next highest number gives us a 1:9 twist.

If anything, the Greenhill formula is a bit on the conservative side, and an optimum twist rate arrived at in this manner is sometimes a bit faster than the industry standard. This is actually not all bad since it is better for the rifling twist rate to be a bit faster than necessary than to be too slow. Benchrest shooters tend to use twist rates on the slow side, and they can get away with doing so since they work only with bullets within an extremely narrow weight range. As for the rest of us, we are better off

INDUSTRY STANDARD RIFLING TWIST RATES

Cartridge	Standard Twist Rate*	Cartridge	Standard Twist Rate*
Rifles		**Rifles**	
.17 Remington	1:9	.30-30 Winchester	1:10, 1:12
.22 Long Rifle	1:16	.300 Savage	1:12
.22 Hornet	1:16**	.308 Winchester	1:12
.218 Bee	1:16	.30-40 Krag	1:10
.219 Zipper	1:14	.30-06 Springfield	1:10
.222 Remington	1:14	.300 H&H Magnum	1:10
.223 Remington	1:7, 1:8, 1:9, 1:10, 1:12***	.300 Norma Magnum	1:10, 1:12
.222 Remington Magnum	1:12, 1:14	.300 Winchester Magnum	1:10
.224 Weatherby Magnum	1:14	.300 Weatherby Magnum	1:10
.225 Winchester	1:14	.30-378 Weatherby Magnum	1:10
.22-250 Remington	1:12, 1:14	.32 Winchester Special	1:16
.220 Swift	1:14	.32 Remington	1:14
.243 Winchester	1:9, 1:10	.338 Winchester Magnum	1:10
.244 Remington	1:9, 1:12****	.340 Weatherby Magnum	1:10
6mm Remington	1:9, 1:10	.33-378 Weatherby Magnum	1:10
.250-3000 Savage	1:10	.348 Winchester	1:12
.257 Roberts	1:10	.35 Remington	1:16
.257 Weatherby Magnum	1:10	.358 Winchester	1:12
6.5x55mm Swedish	1:8, 1:9	.350 Remington Magnum	1:16
6.5 Remington Magnum	1:9	.358 Norma Magnum	1:12
.264 Winchester Magnum	1:9, 1:10	.358 STA	1:12
.270 Winchester	1:10	.375 H&H Magnum	1:12
.270 Weatherby Magnum	1:10	.378 Weatherby Magnum	1:12
7mm-08 Remington	1:9¼	.416 Remington Magnum	1:14
7x57mm Mauser	1:9, 1:9½, 1:10	.416 Rigby	1:14
.284 Winchester	1:9½, 1:10	.416 Weatherby Magnum	1:14
.280 Remington	1:9¼, 1:9½	.44 Remington Magnum	1:38
7mm Remington Magnum	1:9, 1:9½, 1:10	.444 Marlin	1:38
7mm Weatherby Magnum	1:10	.45-70 Government	1:20
7mm STW	1:9, 1:9½	.458 Winchester	1:14
.30 Carbine	1:20	.460 Weatherby Magnum	1:16

* Some companies have standardized on different twist rates than others. For example, the three rates shown for the 7x57mm Mauser are used by FN, Ruger, and Winchester, respectively.

** Some modern rifles in this caliber have quicker twist rates; the Ruger Model 77/22H and its 1:14-inch twist is an example.

*** Twist rates of 1:10 and 1:12 inches are most common while quicker twists are found in rifles in which extremely long bullets, such as the Sierra 69-grain MatchKing, are used.

**** Model 722 rifles built during the last few years of production had the faster 1:9-inch twist that is required for stabilizing 100-grain spitzers.

going with a twist that's a bit too fast because it allows us to use a variety of bullet weights in the same barrel.

I'm convinced that several of the industry-standard twist rates which became established many years ago are a bit too slow for some of the extremely long bullets available today. The .257 Roberts with its 1:10 twist is a good example. Most rifles in that caliber I have worked with were considerably more accurate with bullets weighing 100 grains and less than with heavier bullets. In fact, it has happened often enough to convince me that anyone who wants to shoot the heavier bullets in that cartridge would be wise to choose a twist rate of 1:9 inches, just like the Greenhill formula recommends.

accurately than a light barrel simply because it heats up more slowly during firing. The quicker a barrel heats up the quicker it will begin to warp just enough to affect bullet dispersion from shot to shot. This is not to say that a lightweight barrel can't produce acceptable accuracy, but there is a limit to just how small in diameter it can be.

All barrelmakers offer barrels in a number of weights and contours. For instance, Shilen offers a number of different contours ranging from the No. 1 Featherweight, which, depending on caliber, will finish up in the neighborhood of 2.75 pounds, to the No. 10 Benchrest Special, which can weigh well over eight pounds. Other barrelmakers offer

similar contours, but they can vary in weight by several ounces from shop to shop. A No. 5 contour from Jarrett, for example, weighs a few ounces less than a No. 5 contour from Shilen. Barrels of the same contour from the same company but in different calibers will also vary slightly in weight.

The lightest 22-inch barrels commonly seen on factory rifles measure .500 to .560 inch in diameter at the muzzle, and their weight usually averages around 2.5 pounds. This is typical of barrels on the Winchester Model 70 Featherweight as well as Remington's Model Seven and Model 700 Mountain Rifle. Shilen's Featherweight contour also weighs about the same. While exceptions

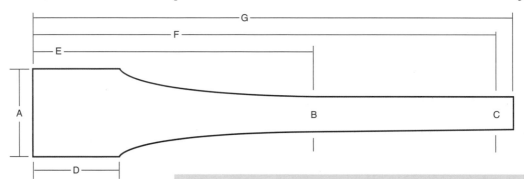

On the other hand, some standard twists are quicker than they really need to be for big-game rifles. While 1:10 has long been standard for the .30-06 and various .300 Magnums, I find that a 1:12 twist works out just as well. Some gunsmiths actually prefer the slower twist for all .30-caliber cartridges. Like I said before, unless you already know for sure what rifling twist rate to specify, it's not a bad idea to leave the decision to your gunsmith or barrelmaker.

Barrel Contours

Given two barrels of equal quality, a heavy barrel will usually shoot more

Shilen Barrel Contour Weights And Dimensions

No./Contour	Dimensions (Inches)							Weight
	A	B	C	D	E	F	G	
1/Featherweight	1.200	.700	0.550	2.5	6	20	22	2 lbs., 10 oz.
2/Lightweight	1.200	.765	0.575	2.5	6	24	26	3 lbs., 3 oz.
3/Sporter	1.200	.815	0.625	2.5	6	24	26	3 lbs., 8 oz.
4/Magnum Sporter	1.200	.860	0.650	3.0	6	26	28	4 lbs., 2 oz.
5/Lt. Wt. Varmint	1.200	.910	0.700	3.0	6	26	28	4 lbs., 8 oz.
5.5/Med. Wt. Varmint	1.200	.960	0.750	3.0	6	26	28	5 lbs.
6/Lt. Wt. Target*	1.250	——	0.750	3.0	-	26	28	6 lbs.
7LV/Lt. Varmint*	1.250	——	0.840	3.0	-	26	28	6 lbs., 12 oz.
7S/Standard Varmint*	1.250	——	0.890	4.0	-	26	28	7 lbs., 1 oz.
7HV/Heavy Varmint*	1.250	——	0.940	5.0	-	26	28	7 lbs., 8 oz.
8/Heavy Bull*	1.200	——	1.000	3.0	-	26	28	7 lbs., 12 oz.
9/Rimfire Target*	1.125	——	0.825	4.0	-	26	28	5 lbs., 12 oz.
10/BR Special	——	——	Straight cylinder, 1.30 to 1.40 inches diameter					
11/Straight	——	——	Any diameter up to 1.230 inches					

*Straight taper

NOTES: Dimension "C" is the muzzle diameter at dimension "F," which is Shilen's recommended finish length although the barrel can be finished shorter. Different caliber will vary slightly in weight with each contour.

will exist, I believe those barrels represent about the lightest that are capable of approaching minute of angle for three shots at 100 yards on a consistent basis. Even then the barrel must be top-quality, it must be installed properly, and it's best to keep bore size at 7mm or smaller since within a particular contour the larger the bore of a barrel the quicker it will heat up during firing.

When it comes to big-game rifles chambered for magnum cartridges, I have had the best luck with more beef in their barrels. My standard-weight Model 700 in .257 STW, which was built by Lex Weberneck of Rifles Inc., has a Shilen No. 4 barrel, and it will consistently average less than half an inch for three shots at 100 yards. My most accurate rifle in 7mm STW is also capable of half-minute-of-angle accuracy, and it wears a No. 4 Hart barrel. The most accurate big-game rifle in .30-378 Weatherby Magnum I have ever fired was built by Jarrett using one of his No. 5 barrels. Keep in

mind now, I'm talking about rifles capable of averaging half-minute of angle and better. If less accuracy is acceptable, then a lighter barrel will certainly do. I have a Remington 700 with an extremely lightweight barrel in .375 H&H Magnum, and while it doesn't come close to shooting minute-of-angle-size groups, it is a joy to tote in rough country and plenty accurate for bumping off a brown bear or Cape buffalo.

As for a varmint rifle chambered for one of the .22-, .24-, or .25-caliber cartridges, Shilen's No. 5 contour or a barrel of similar weight from another maker is probably the minimum that should be used if consistent half-minute-of-angle accuracy is desired. This is for a rifle that will be used for more walking than sitting. When sitting in one spot and shooting all day long I'd just as soon have an even heavier barrel. In fact, the muzzles on some of my favorite sitting rifles range in diameter from .720 inch for a Model 700 with a Jarrett barrel in .223 to .940 inch for a 40-XBR with a factory barrel in .220 Swift.

When rebarreling a rifle or building a custom rifle from scratch its final weight can be adjusted either up or down by choosing the right barrel contour. Making an accurate projection of what a finished rifle will weigh boils down to a simple matter of adding up the weights of its component parts. Let's say you're thinking about having a Winchester Model 70 rebarreled and want to know how much it will weigh with

NOMINAL TURNBOLT ACTION WEIGHTS	
(To Be Used In Projecting Finished Rifle Weight)	
Action	Weight (Ounces)
Browning BBR	50.9
1917 Enfield	48.2
1898 Mauser	45.2
Remington Models 600/660/XP-100	31.4
Remington Models 700/721 (standard action)	38.1
Remington Models 700/722 (short action)	35.2
Remington Model 788	43.2
Ruger Model 77 (short action)	37.8
Ruger Model 77 (long action)	40.8
Sako L461 (small, .222-size action)	32.7
Savage Model 110/112 (short action)	37.5
Savage Model 110C/112C (short action)	39.1
Savage Model 110/112 (long action)	37.5
1903 Springfield	44.3
Weatherby Magnum Mark V	50.5
Weatherby Lightweight Mark V	40.5
Weatherby Mark V Varmintmaster	31.3
Winchester Model 70 Standard (Pre-'64)	45.5
Winchester Model 70 Featherweight (Pre-'64)	42.6
Winchester Model 70 Standard (Post-'64)	44.3

NOTES: Weights shown are for complete action including receiver, bolt, trigger group, and magazine/floorplate assembly.

the barrel you like before you actually place an order for the barrel. First weigh the stock, scope, and scope mount and then add what you get to the weight of the Model 70 action shown in the accompanying action weight chart. Then add the weight of the new barrel and you've got it. As illustrated by the Shilen barrel contour chart I have included in this report, most barrelmakers list both weights and dimensions for the various contours they offer. If, after adding everything up, your projected weight of the rifle is lighter or heavier than you're shooting for, simply go with a heavier or lighter barrel contour.

The same type of finished weight projection is just as easily done when building a custom rifle from scratch except you'll have to contact other manufacturers and obtain the weights of other items such as the

Given two barrels of equal quality, a heavy one is likely to be more accurate than a thin one because it heats up more slowly during firing.

Barrel Grades

Aftermarket rifle barrels are available in three basic levels of quality from various makers. Different barrelmakers give them different names, so to keep it simple I'll refer to them as utility grade, standard grade, and benchrest grade. The three grades of barrels may look the same on the outside, but they differ inside where it's important.

Least expensive of the group is the utility-grade barrel. This is the barrel for the fellow who simply wants to put together a good shooter and is satisfied with less than tackhole accuracy. Some barrelmakers, such as Wilson Arms Co. and Small Arms Mfg. Co. (formerly E. R. Shaw Inc.), specialize in utility-grade barrels. While this grade cannot be expected to produce the same accuracy as a barrel costing twice as much, it is certainly adequate for some applications. Some barrels of this type can be surprisingly accurate; a Wilson barrel in .223 I once shot averaged around 0.70 inch for five-shot groups while a .30-06 barrel from E. R. Shaw would consistently keep five bullets inside 1.25 inches at 100 yards.

Some shops offer several grades of barrels while others offer only one. From Shilen you can buy what that company calls its Lone Star, Match, and Select Match grades, the latter used to break all sorts of accuracy records by benchrest shooters. Other shops, such as Lilja, Schneider, Jarrett, Krieger, H-S Precision, and Gaillard, offer only benchrest-grade barrels.

To understand the major difference between the three grades of barrels you must first understand that the most important characteristic that determines the accuracy of a barrel is the uniformity of its bore and groove diameters. In other words, in order for a barrel to be capable of extremely good accuracy, the bore and groove diameters of its rifling must be quite uniform from one end to the other. Other factors can affect accuracy to a lesser degree, but the single most important is dimensional uniformity. To illustrate the internal dimensional differences in three different grades of barrels, I'll describe those made by Shilen.

On its least expensive Lone Star Grade barrel, Shilen maintains a bore diameter uniformity variation of no more than .0005 inch and holds groove diameter to within .001 inch. To a machinist those tolerances might seem quite generous, but they are tighter than the typical mass-produced barrel made by most of the major rifle manufacturers.

Moving on up to a slightly higher level of precision, a barrel must have a bore and groove diameter unifor-

An air gauge is often used by top barrelmakers to measure the dimensional uniformity of bore and groove diameters.

mity of .0003 inch before Shilen will stamp it "Match Grade."

Then we have Shilen's Select Match Grade barrel (which I commonly describe as benchrest-grade); its maximum bore and groove diameter variation is a mere .0001. All Jarrett barrels are held to that same .0001-inch tolerance, and the same holds true for benchrest-grade barrels made by Schneider and Lilja. What this means is, if the groove diameter of the rifling in, say, a .30-caliber barrel starts out at .3080 inch at its breech end, it cannot measure more than .3081 inch at any point within the length of the barrel from the chamber to the muzzle. Same goes for bore diameter. If that same .30-caliber barrel starts out with a bore diameter of .300 inch, it cannot measure more than .3001 inch at any point. To put this into its proper perspective, a single page in the typical gun magazine is .002 inch thick. If it were possible to separate one of those pages into 20 separate layers, all measuring precisely the same, the thickness of one of those layers would measure the same as the maximum bore and groove diameter variation in a benchrest-grade barrel.

Incidentally, the bore and groove diameters of a barrel are measured by an expensive device called an air gauge. It works by pumping a constant stream of air through a long hollow rod that has a plug on its end with holes through which the air flows. The plug is a close fit with the bore of the barrel, and a different one is used for each caliber. Any variations in resistance to the air escaping through the plug is indicated by a steel ball that rides on a column of air inside a graduated glass cylinder. As the plug is pushed through the barrel, air pressure on the ball remains constant if bore and groove diameters are extremely uniform from one end of the barrel to the other. If not, more air will escape

Barrelmakers often scrap barrels that don't meet their established accuracy level.

through the plug as it passes over an oversized area in the barrel, and this is indicated by movement of the steel ball inside the gauge.

Getting back to making an extremely accurate benchrest-grade barrel, in order to achieve such a high level of uniformity, the bore and groove diameters of its rifling must first be machined slightly undersized and then carefully hand-lapped to the desired dimensions. This takes lots of time, and, as we all know, time is money in any business. Pat Moore, who makes the barrels for Jarrett Rifles, tells me that four barrels are the maximum he can hand-lap on one of his better eight-hour workdays.

And what happens to a barrel that doesn't qualify internally as benchrest-grade? It depends on the barrelmaker. Some downgrade it to a lower level and sell it for less money. Others wring their hands and cry out in sadness as they toss it into the scrap heap. The last time I visited Jarrett Rifles, I noticed a couple of steel drums full of rejects, any one of which was probably capable of averaging well under an inch. By now you should be starting to understand why a top-of-line benchrest-grade barrel is more expensive than other grades.

Is a benchrest-grade barrel worth its extra cost? Probably not to the shooter who is content with less accuracy than it can deliver. On the other hand, the more expensive barrel is most definitely worth the extra money to a benchrest competitor since a rifle that isn't capable of consistently shooting five shots into less than 0.200 inch at 100 yards won't cut it in that game. A top-grade barrel is also worth the extra money to the big-game hunter or varmint shooter who enjoys shooting groups measuring less than half-minute of angle. From a practical point of view, that shooter may not actually need such a high level of accuracy, but having it at his disposal makes him more confident in his ability to hit distant targets.

Before leaving the subject, I must mention that a standard-grade barrel that comes mighty close to equaling the accuracy of a benchrest-grade barrel does occasionally come along, and I have been fortunate enough to own a couple. But such a barrel comes as a result of luck of the draw and is not something that can be counted on. This is another reason why some shooters are convinced that buying a top-quality barrel is money well spent. If during the next few years you bought several utility-grade or standard-grade barrels from a particular shop, all chambered for the same cartridge, chances are slim that their accuracy would be the same. Each and every one of those barrels might prove satisfactory to you, but chances are good their accuracy would vary. In contrast, if those were genuine benchrest-grade barrels from a reputable shop, their accuracy would more than likely be virtually identical. This is why some gunsmiths who specialize in building super-accurate rifles for varmint shooting, big-game hunting, benchrest competition, and long-range target shooting refuse to use anything but top-quality barrels. When they build a rifle that doesn't shoot to their expectations, having used the best barrel money can buy eliminates one of the possible causes.

Standard Versus Tight-Necked Chambers

A tight-necked chamber or a chamber with an undersized neck requires the turning of all case necks before they can be fired in the rifle. This is not a bad deal for a benchrest shooter who will probably wear out the barrel on his rifle with no more than a dozen cases. But on a varmint rifle it is a pain in the posterior since far more cases are required. This holds especially true for a rifle to be used for shooting prairie dogs. A tight-necked chamber is also a terrible choice for a big-game rifle since it won't accept factory ammo. I absolutely will not have this type of chamber on a rifle that is to be used for anything other than competitive benchrest shooting, and I base this opinion on far more than mere speculation. Over the years I have compared the accuracy of a number of heavy-barrel varmint rifles and have yet to find that a tight-necked chamber squeezes down group size enough to notice. It might be important to a benchrest shooter who must do everything humanly possible to make his rifle shoot inside 0.200 inch at 100 yards, but for everyone else the inconvenience far outweighs any possible gain.

BETTER MARKSMANSHIP

By Richard Mann

A good field shot is a combination of good equipment and skill. Money can get the equipment, but you must put in the hours of practice time. The end result will be worth the effort.

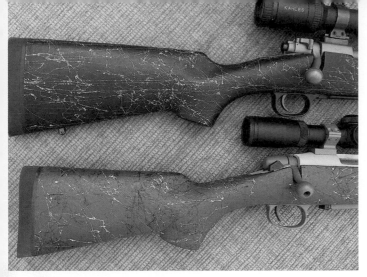

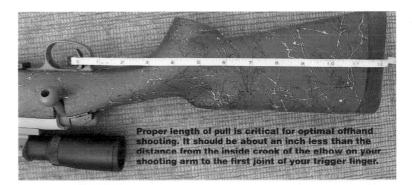

Proper length of pull is critical for optimal offhand shooting. It should be about an inch less than the distance from the inside crook of the elbow on your shooting arm to the first joint of your trigger finger.

al respected shooting academies across the country offer courses on the hunting rifle. They are expensive but can be worth attending if graduates make perfecting the skills presented them a priority. We learn physical skills by doing, or by trial and error, not by instruction.

We all like to think that we have a little Ned Roberts in us—usually more than actually exists. I'm not saying hunters are poor marksmen but that on average hunters think they are better rifle shots than they really are. Every year I conduct a rifle workshop for one of the top custom rifle builders in the country where hunters are invited to test their shooting skills in simulated hunting conditions. Even experienced hunters perform well below their expectations—most often with an excuse for every miss.

Major Ned Roberts, designer of the .257 Roberts cartridge, was lucky. Roberts's Uncle Bud taught him how to shoot a rifle. Uncle Bud was an accomplished shot and had been a member of Berdan's Sharpshooters, during the Civil War. When Roberts was not yet a teenager, Uncle Bud started him on a rigorous practice regime, and before long Roberts was able to put four out of five shots inside a two-inch bullseye at 55 yards using a .30-caliber muzzleloader and open sights from the standing, offhand position. After Roberts accomplished that feat, the range and target size were doubled. After Roberts managed to qualify at 165 yards with the same proficiency, Uncle Bud proclaimed him a good shot with a rifle. The year was 1876, and Roberts was not yet 10. That same year he shot his first big-game animal: a lynx that weighed 67 pounds. Things were different in 1886. In those days marksmanship was considered as important as good manners and good grades.

Most of us are not lucky enough to have an Uncle Bud, but sever-

Know Your Equipment

Becoming a good field shot is simply a culmination of using good equipment, developing skill, and understanding limitations. Money and good sense will outfit you with the proper equipment, but it takes diligence on your part to feed the monster called practice that most of us ignore.

For starters, rifle fit is very important. Trying to manage a rifle that does not fit you is like wearing boots two sizes too large on a forced road march. Length of pull,

the distance from the rifle's butt to the trigger, is a key measurement and can be adjusted by shortening or lengthening the stock. This is the reason that some firearms manufacturers, such as Remington and Ruger, now offer "youth" rifles that have stocks with a shorter length of pull. These rifles are much more appropriate for youngsters, many women, and small-framed adults.

A rifle that balances behind the front of the action will handle smoothly, and a rifle that balances forward of the action will hang on target better. A compromise is a rifle that balances very near the front of the action, provides good handling characteristics, and a reasonable steadiness on target. The balance point can be adjusted by adding weight to the front or rear of the stock or by shortening the barrel. A rifle's balance is critical for good offhand shooting.

Total rifle weight can influence performance, particularly when shooting offhand. Most rifles will shoot best when total weight is between 6.5 to eight pounds. If total weight is under 6.5 pounds, consider a rifle that is a bit muzzle heavy. If weight is over eight pounds, consider a rifle that is a tad butt heavy. Custom rifle builders I have interviewed—like Melvin Forbes at New Ultra Light Arms and Charlie Sisk at Sisk Rifles—all agree the physical interaction between shooter and rifle is paramount to mastering the fundamentals of field shooting. A rifle needs to fit the shooter and be comfortable to shoot in a variety of positions.

The trigger is even more important. It's the "go" switch and must allow surgical-like manipulation. For about a hundred bucks most triggers can be tuned by a gunsmith, and for most bolt-action rifles, quality replacement triggers, like those from Timney, are available and are usually easy to install.

Proprioception and Kinesthesia

Proprioception is how the body immediately varies muscle contraction in response to external forces and vision. Kinesthesia is the sensation of joint motion and acceleration. Proprioception and kinesthesia are the mechanisms for control and posture of the body. They are what let us shoot accurately. Repeating the same action 3000 to 5000 times, or performing a task approximately 30 minutes for a period of 21 days, is necessary to create muscle memory so that a physical activity can be performed, seemingly without conscious thought. It is cost prohibitive for a shooter to fire that many shots a month. This makes dry fire viable for allowing proprioception and kinesthesia to flourish. In short, it trains your eye to pull the trigger.

Take about 20 minutes out of each day for dry-fire practice. Use an unloaded rifle and a target that will let you observe your sight alignment at the moment the trigger breaks. By the end of a week

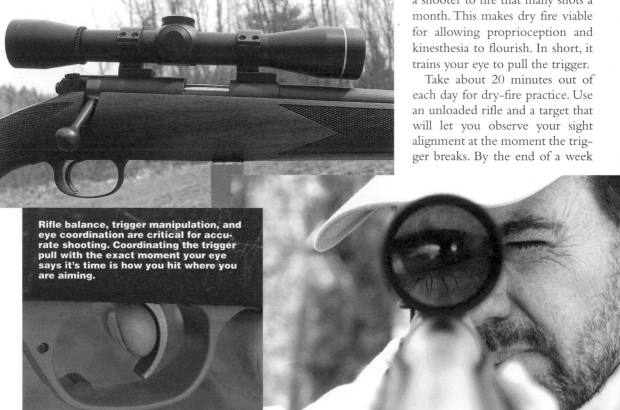

Rifle balance, trigger manipulation, and eye coordination are critical for accurate shooting. Coordinating the trigger pull with the exact moment your eye says it's time is how you hit where you are aiming.

you will start to feel where the sight was orientated on the target when the trigger breaks.

A cliché that is repeated by firearms instructors and others claiming to be masters of the art of shooting is, "It should be a surprise when the rifle fires." Not true. A shooter should know the exact moment when the rifle will fire.

Learning to dictate the exact moment the trigger will break and coordinating that moment with the instant the sight is properly aligned is the key to accurate shooting. It's all about the eye and the trigger.

Before you can improve your shooting you must establish your current ability. Zero your rifle at 50 yards then select a visible target about six to eight inches in diam-

eter and place it at that distance. From the standing, offhand position fire five shots. Take your time, lowering the rifle between each shot, but try to complete all five shots in 60 seconds. Do this three more times for a total of four five-shot groups. The average group size is your score.

For the next week conduct daily dry-fire practice. During weekly

Positioning your shooting arm parallel to the ground wedges the stock between your shoulder and cheek and provides a more stable offhand shooting platform.

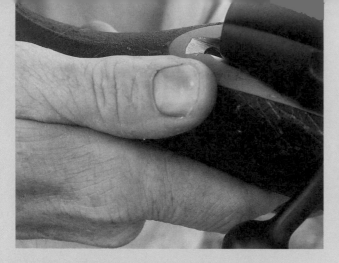

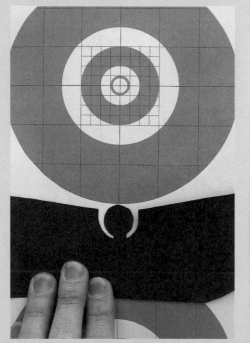

Seven Steps to Better Shooting

1. Do you jerk the trigger? Adjust the grip of your shooting hand so that your thumb doesn't wrap around the wrist of the stock. Sometimes eliminating your ability to "grip" the stock will solve the problem.

2. Riflescope magnification higher than 6X can hinder offhand shooting. If you have trouble seeing the target with low magnification, get a bigger target.

3. Coarse open sights can be difficult to align on a target. Use a six o' clock hold: hold at the bottom of the target. This provides a much more defined aiming point with open sights.

4. To help steady the rifle, raise your shooting elbow so it is parallel to the ground or at a 90-degree angle to your body. This will pinch the rifle between your shoulder and cheek providing a rigid shooting platform.

5. The best offhand shot I know often says, "If you hold long, you hold wrong." Don't struggle to hold a position for more than eight or 10 seconds. If you haven't fired by then, lower the rifle and relax.

6. Do most of your live fire practice with a quality rimfire. It will save money and help overcome flinching.

7. To avoid fatigue, never shoot more than 20 to 30 rounds per live fire session.

range sessions work to reduce your average group size by a half-inch or a full inch each time out until you reach your goal—whatever it may be. Then double the range like Uncle Bud did with Ned and keep practicing until you are shooting groups no more than double the size you were shooting at 50 yards. Keep up the dry-fire practice, and if your ability starts to fall off, go back to 50 yards and start over.

An excellent rifleman can put five shots inside a one-inch cir-cle at 50 yards from the standing offhand position. A very good marksman will do the same in-side a two-inch circle, and if you can keep four out of five shots in-side a two-inch circle at 50 yards, consider yourself a good shot and ready to square off against old Ned Roberts.

Don't overlook target selection. Select a target that is easy to see and not too small. Itty-bitty circles and squares are made for shooting from a bench, so use robust targets for offhand training. The target creates the visual impression your eye relies on to signal your finger to activate the trigger.

In short, make sure your rifle fits you, make sure your trigger is crisp, and practice, practice, practice! The end result will be worth the effort. When in the field you will have the experience to help you decide what shots you should take and the confidence in your equipment and ability to make the ones you do.

ACCURACY FACT-POWDER CHARGES

BY LAYNE SIMPSON

Some handloaders seem convinced that in order to achieve the best accuracy, all powder charges must weigh exactly the same. While precisely weighed charges certainly don't hurt anything, they often contribute very little to accuracy when com-pared to other influencing factors. It's impossible to say what exact percentage of weight variation in a powder charge will begin to affect accuracy, but most rifles won't indicate a great difference in group size until powder charge weight varies by 1 percent. This would amount to two or three tenths of a grain with small cartridges like the .222 Remington and a full grain or more with big boomers like the .300 Kong (.30-378 Improved).

I've shot some rifles chambered for the big car-tridges that indicated absolutely no difference in accuracy between precisely weighed powder charges and those that varied by as much as 2 percent.

What does seem to affect accuracy is powder charge density. Handloads with powders that fill the case to 100 percent density or close to it are usually more accurate than those of less density, but there are exceptions. When combined with the right bullets, some of the faster-burning propellants produce excel-lent accuracy even when occupying only a small per-centage of the powder cavity in the case.

Classic .45 ACP loads used by bullseye competitors to rack up high scores for many decades have con-sisted of 3.3 to 3.5 grains of Bullseye behind various cast bullets. Relatively mild charges of IMR-4895 in the .30-06 have won many long-range matches, and charges of W748 used by those who compete with the .308 Winchester don't even come close to filling the cases.

Several years ago I attended the Coors Schuetzen-fest in Golden, Colorado, and those chaps taught me how accurate tiny, low-density powder charges and cast bullets can be. As a rule, extremely slow-burning propellants produce better accuracy when loaded at close to full density. This especially holds true for the spherical types, which should never be loaded below 90-percent density. But many other propellants with fast to medium burn rates produce excellent accuracy when loaded to densities far below 100 percent.

LONG-RANGE MILITARY ACCURACY

By David M. Fortier
PHOTOS BY EMILY K. FORTIER

For decades the U.S. military has been applying advanced techniques and technology learned through rifle competition to the battlefield.

10

X

SOLDIER
RESULTS

@ 1000YDS

It was one of those hot August days in sunny Georgia. You know the type, the ones best spent around air conditioning, leisurely sipping on some sweet tea. Unfortunately both air conditioning and sweet tea were in regrettably short supply on Fort Stewart's 900-meter sniper range. Looking up from my spotting scope, I wiped away the beads of sweat running down the lenses of my glasses and glanced towards George, the Civilian Marksmanship Instructor to my right. George was as hot as I was, but he seemed oblivious to it. He was watching mirage through his spotting scope like a cat watches a mouse. Lying prone to his right and left were two young troopers from the 3/7th Cav. Both were behind Army Marksmanship Unit-built Squad Designated Marksman Rifles (SDM-Rs) and were carefully aiming at silhouettes on the 800-meter line. Now, 800 meters is a long shot indeed for a 5.56mm M16. It's actually some 300 meters farther than the SDM-R is realistically intended for. Despite this minor fact, George, without taking his

eye from his spotting scope, prodded the foot of the trooper on his left and said, "Hold center, left edge."

"Center, left edge," the E-2 replied.

"Send it," George said curtly, watching through his scope. Glancing into my Nikon's eyepiece I watched the round's trace as it arched high and then dropped, knocking the "Ivan" pop-up target flat. George's stone-faced expression immediately broke into a grin. "Nice shot, very well done, Rossetti. Now give me another one." Before they were done Private Rossetti, and several other students in the Designated Marksman class, had made hits on man-sized targets all the way out to the range's limit—900 meters. What made this all the more impressive was that very few, if any, of the students in the two-day class had ever previously shot past 300 meters.

What at first glance seems to be simply a fine display of military marksmanship reveals more under closer examination. The students were indeed all young cavalry troopers from Apache, Bonecrusher, and Crazy-

horse troops of the 3/7th Cav. who were preparing for deployment to Iraq. However, their SDM-Rs were designed and built using accuracy lessons learned from NRA High Power competition. Indeed, even their stone-faced civilian instructor George had been a member of the vaunted Marine Corps Rifle Team during a previous life. He had learned the fine art of long-range shooting behind a National Match M14, in interservice competition. Now he was sharing the practical aspects of his knowledge to help these young soldiers improve their accuracy in order to fight terrorism.

Although many, especially in the military, fail to grasp the importance of a healthy competitive marksmanship program, time and time again it has proven vitally important to the defense of our great country. While it is true that competitive rifle shooting is a useful tool for teaching the foundational skills of marksmanship, it actually does much more than just that. Through the decades lessons learned in competition have led directly to advances in techniques and technology that were then applied to the battlefield. This includes both ammunition and rifles.

As an example, the primary mission of the Army Marksmanship Unit (AMU) is competitive shooting. However, due to its expertise in this area it has also developed and tested the M14 National Match rifle, M21 sniper rifle, M24 sniper rifle, and the new Squad Designated Marksman Rifle. In addition, the AMU laid the groundwork for both accurizing the M16 and developing heavy 5.56mm match loads. Generally, when precision rifles are being built for either competition or combat in the military, the same gunsmiths are involved in both programs. So the crossover of technology is to be expected.

One prime example of this is the ammunition fielded by Army and Marine Corps snipers. Field use of match ammunition originally intended for competition has long been an accepted practice among military snipers. While standard military ball ammunition can be surprisingly accurate, it all too often is rather ho-hum in this regard due to manufacturing tolerances and quality control. As an example, the current accuracy standard for M855 ball ammunition to be accepted is just 4 MOA. In addition, the projectile design of standard military ammunition is seldom optimized for use at the long ranges over which a sniper plies his trade.

Match ammunition developed specifically for across-the-course and long-range competition, on the other hand, is a different animal entirely. Carefully crafted to produce consistently tight groups at long range, this ammunition is designed for one purpose: to win. The cartridge cases, primers, powder, and projectiles are all held to tighter tolerances. Streamlined projectiles with higher than average ballistic coefficients are also usually utilized to provide less wind drift at long range. The end result is a highly accurate cartridge that is at home punching Xs at 600 or 1000 yards. As to be expected, the attributes of a match cartridge are very similar to those required by a military sniper.

The first .30-caliber match ammunition loaded for the U.S. military that I am aware of was a run made by Remington in 1907. Unfortunately, the specific loading has been lost to time, but we do know it was expressly made for, and used in, the Palma Match that year. Although the accuracy of this first lot is unknown, we do have some data on later years. As an example, a 180-grain cupronickel flatbase bullet was loaded by U.S.C.C.O. for the 1908 Olympics. This "International" load grouped into a mean radius of just 2.81 inches at 600 yards. Frankford Arsenal's ammunition was selected for the 1909 National Matches. Loaded with a M1906 150-grain FMJ, this special run had a mean radius of 4.92 inches at 600 yards. During the pre-World War I years, match ammunition was

slowly refined and improved for the then-new .30-06 cartridge. While this ammunition was intended solely for competition, 100,000 rounds of match ammunition loaded with 180-grain bullets was ordered during World War I. Part of this lot was shipped to Europe for combat use.

Competition being what it is, efforts were constantly made to improve the accuracy and consistency of these special ammunition runs. A substantial step forward came with the development of a 173-grain FMJ projectile with a 9-degree boattail and gilding metal jacket. Loaded into ammunition for the 1925 National Matches by Frankford Arsenal, this load grouped into a mean radius of just 2.3 inches at 600 yards. A similar load with a longer overall length than service rifle ammunition for Palma use provided a mean radius of just 4.43 inches at 1000 yards. This projectile, manufactured to looser tolerances, was subsequently adopted in 1926 as Cal. .30 Ball Cartridge, M1. For decades subsequent military match ammunition was based upon this projectile design.

Without a doubt quantities of the pre-war match ammunition also saw combat during World War II. I know of one tale of two crusty old Marine Corps NCOs landing on a Japanese-held island in the Pacific wearing shooting jackets and Smoky the Bear

hats. When machine gun fire from a distant pillbox brought a halt to the advance, a call went out, "Sniper up!" A short time later these two Marines sauntered up and rolled out their shooting mats as if they were at Camp Perry. Then one got behind a spotting scope while the other flopped behind a Unertl-topped M1903 Springfield. With his spotter calling corrections via bullet trace, the old Marine rifleman, despite it being over 1000 yards away, knocked a chunk of concrete from the pillbox on his second shot. Making windage corrections as he went, he then proceeded to move his point of impact from the left edge to the center of the pillbox where the machine gun was. Within a few rounds he began to drop 173-grain FMJ-BTs through the narrow firing slit with monotonous regularity until the Japanese machine gun spoke no more. The two old NCOs then rolled up their shooting mats and proceeded to where they were needed next. I suspect the ammunition they carried that day was from a favorite lot they had shot in competition.

Although the M1 ball round was replaced by the lighter M2 ball round on January 12, 1940, the projectile was simply too good to die. It was subsequently resurrected during development of the M72 .30-caliber match cartridge. This load was introduced in 1957 for the National Matches and

Developed for match competition, the .30-06 M72 Match round was used effectively by military snipers in Vietnam.

The 7.62mm M118 Match ammunition was also developed for competition use (in the M14 National Match rifle) but was later used by U.S. snipers.

launched its 173-grain FMJ projectile at 2640 fps. Highly successful in competition, it came packed in either eight-round Garand clips or 20-round cardboard boxes. Later in the 1960s this load was widely used by M1D and Model 70-equipped snipers in Vietnam to turn live VC into good VC. It was this load that Carlos Hathcock, himself a highly successful competition shooter, used with such telling effect on the VC and NVA.

Having grown long in the tooth, the .30-06 cartridge was eventually replaced in U.S. service by the 7.62x51mm. This led to the development and adoption of the 7.62mm M118 Match cartridge in 1965. Intended for use in the then-new M14 National Match rifle, it was loaded with the same 173-grain FMJ bullet as used previously in M72 Match ammunition. The main difference was a slightly slower velocity of 2550 fps. The result was a highly accurate load that performed well in competition, remaining supersonic past 1000 yards. It wasn't long before M14 National Match rifles loaded with M118 Match ammunition had bested the older M1 National Match and M72 combo in competition. Due to its accuracy it was soon fielded with the M14-based M21 sniper rifle in Vietnam. Put to the test of combat, this FMJ match load proved a valuable asset thanks to its accuracy and

penetration. Unlike the 5.56mm M193 ball round riflemen were equipped with, the 7.62mm M118 penetrated foliage and light cover easily. It went on to remain standard issue for decades.

Unfortunately, the post-Vietnam era was hard on the military. Funding was cut, and troops made do with what was available. By the 1980s, due to worn bulletmaking machinery and poor quality control at Lake City Army Ammunition Plant, the accuracy of M118 had dropped considerably. It eventually lost its Match designation and was redesignated simply Special Ball. Due to mediocre accuracy, military rifle teams were forced to pull the military FMJ-BT projectile and replace it with a 168-grain Sierra MatchKing to remain competitive. Dubbed "Mexican Match," this practice remained common until a new Match load, the M852, became widely available. In a departure from the past, the new load was topped with a commercial HPBT bullet— Sierra's famous 168-grain MatchKing. Although FMJ-BT projectiles can be quite accurate, the manufacturing process of HPBTs produces a more consistent and thus more accurate projectile.

Although extremely accurate at shorter ranges, the M852 did have one shortcoming. It would not reliably remain supersonic to 1000 yards. Prominently marked "Not for Combat Use,"

the M852 was intended for competition only while the M118 Special Ball soldiered on for sniping. Eventually dissatisfaction with the M118 SB, combined with experience using the M852 and its commercial HPBT projectile, led to the development of a new sniper load. Designated the M118 Long Range, this new load was topped with a brand-new 175-grain Sierra MatchKing projectile. Similar in profile and ballistic coefficient to the old 173-grain FMJ-BT projectile, the new 175-grain Match-King provided superior accuracy all the way to 1000 yards. Adopted in the late 1990s, the M118LR remains standard issue to our snipers and has performed well in actual combat. It's interesting to note, though, that this round would be as at home punching Xs on the 600-yard line at Camp Perry as punching terrorists from a rooftop in Fallujah.

The lessons gleaned from competition shooting are even more apparent when it comes to 5.56mm ammunition. Up until the 1990s the 7.62mm M14 National Match basically ruled Service Rifle competition. At this time the M16A1/A2 was considered something of an oddity in Service Rifle competition. Although accurate and light recoiling on the short lines, it wasn't competitive at 600 yards due to the available projectiles. This all changed when the Army Marksmanship Unit began work on turning the M16A2 into a viable competition rifle. A large part of this process was developing suitable loads for use at 600 yards. When Sierra introduced 77- and 80-grain Match-King HPBTs a suitably modified M16 suddenly became hard to beat, even by an M14. When the M16-wielding AMU proceeded to thrash the vaunted M14-toting Marine Corps Rifle Team it became painfully obvious the sun had finally set on the M14 National Match rifle for competition.

When a suitable 5.56mm sniper load was required for use in SOCOM's new Mk12 series of sniper rifles it was simply based directly upon existing match ammunition. Manufactured exclusively

Current M14-based sniper rifles, like this one being used in Afghanistan, benefit from decades of accurizing techniques learned in rifle match shooting.

Military Match Ammo Velocity

Military Load	Velocity (fps)
.30-06	
M72 Match 173-gr. FMJ-BT	2640
7.62mm NATO	
M118 Match 173-gr. FMJ-BT	2550
M852 Match 168-gr. HPBT	2550
M118 Long Range 175-gr. HPBT	2550

(Photo Courtesy of U.S. Army)

by Black Hills Ammunition for the military, this new load was designed to provide both enhanced accuracy and terminal performance at extended distances. When development work on this load first began, a 73-grain Berger Open Tip Match bullet was originally selected. However, this was soon changed to a 77-grain Sierra MatchKing, which is still loaded today. To enhance its exterior ballistics and terminal performance this ammunition is loaded to higher 5.56 NATO pressures. The resulting cartridge is very similar to Match ammunition loaded for the Army Marksmanship Unit for use in competition.

The Mk12's dedicated ammunition evolved and was eventually type classified as MK262 Mod 0. Combat experience soon led to this load evolving into its present MK262 Mod 1 configuration. The primary, but not only, difference between the two types is the addition of a cannelure to the Mod 1 projectile to prevent bullet set-back during feeding. Both terminal performance and accuracy of this ammunition is markedly improved over M855 ball. Each lot is tested for accuracy by firing 10 10-shot groups at 300 yards. The average group size is between 2.00 and 2.50 inches. Unlike the 62-grain M855 ball round, the 77-grain Sierra MatchKing fragments much more reliably out to much longer distances. This dramatically increases terminal performance. The downside is that penetration, especially on hard targets, is not as good as the M855 round. In actual combat the MK262 Mod 1 proved very effective, and it quickly made a name for itself. It wasn't long before it became a desirable commodity, being used by whatever troops could get their hands on it.

For the civilian shooter interested in building handloads that duplicate the ballistic performance of these military loads, the chore is not a difficult one. It simply takes matching the correct projectile to a quality case, like a Winchester, and loading it to the proper velocity. .30-06 M2 ball can be dupli-

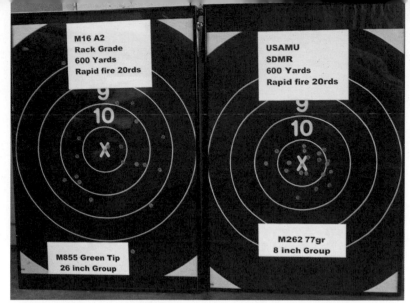

The lessons learned from competition shooting are even more apparent when it comes to 5.56mm ammunition. By developing extremely accurate ammunition, the AMU turned the M16A2 into a viable 600-yard competition rifle, and the ammunition was quickly adapted for sniper use.

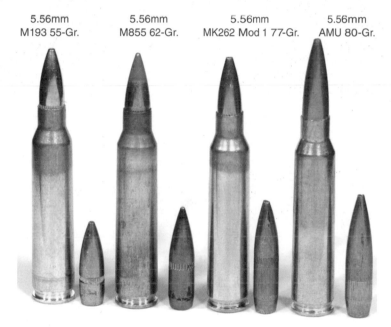

cated using a Prvi Partizan 150-grain FMJ bullet available from Graf & Sons. M72 Match ammunition is a bit harder. Prvi Partizan does make a correct 173-grain FMJ-BT, but it can be difficult to find. I suggest simply replacing it with a Sierra 175-grain MatchKing. M118LR is easily duplicated using Sierra's 175-grain MatchKing.

When loading the .30 calibers simply pick one of the many suitable medium-burning powders. To duplicate the MK262 Mod 1 load a 77-grain Sierra MatchKing but stay on the safe side regarding velocity. Mil-Spec MK 262 Mod 1 is loaded very hot using powder not commercially available to reloaders. So don't try to match the velocity.

How to Shoot for ACCURACY

EVERY SERIOUS RIFLEMAN HAS HIS OWN PROCEDURE FOR ACCURACY-TESTING RIFLES. HERE'S HOW OUR MATCH-WINNING, WORLD-WIDE-HUNTING, VENERABLE FIELD EDITOR DOES IT.

BY LAYNE SIMPSON

The accuracy-testing protocol for rifles has varied considerably through the years, not only among individual shooters, but also among the various types of shooting activities. It also is subject to being changed from time to time.

During the 1950s, National Rifle Association personnel often fired three-shot groups and allowed the barrel to cool down one minute between each shot. That protocol has since changed to five-shot groups with no barrel cooling between shots. A friend of mine fires three-shot groups and allows the barrel to cool down two minutes between each shot. Another shoots five-shot groups and gives the barrel five minutes to cool between shots. The author of a test report I read several years ago fired five shots but measured only the closest three holes in the target for record. As I said, it varies.

Like most shooters, I have my own procedure for checking the accuracy of rifles. It remains the same regardless of whether the testing is done for my own information or for publication. It is also the same for rifles owned by me as well as those received on consignment from the various manufacturers for evaluation. This is not to say my methods are better than those used by others, and I am not implying that others should

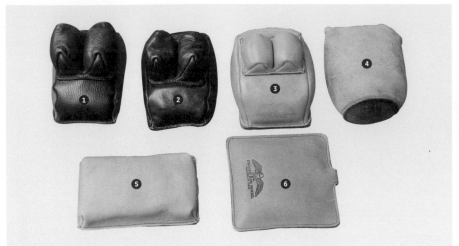

follow them. What I am saying is they have worked satisfactorily for me for several decades, and I see no reason for changing.

The Ammunition

When testing a new rifle, I almost always start by shooting factory ammunition if it is available. I do this because factory technicians are quite good at developing loads capable of delivering levels of accuracy ranging from acceptable to excellent when fired in a large number of mass-produced rifles from various manufacturers.

The level of accuracy may not be as good as I will eventually achieve through trial-and-error handloading for a specific rifle, but it gives me something to shoot

The sissy bag is too thick to place between the shooter's shoulder and the butt of a riflestock, so it is positioned on its side. Placing it on a brick bag elevates it to the proper position.

for and to possibly improve on. If the cartridge a particular rifle is chambered for is available with match bullets, I try to shoot at least one of those loads. Due to excellent match loadings of the .308 Winchester from Black Hills and Federal, I love it when a rifle to be tested is chambered for that cartridge.

The Number of Shots

The rifle to be tested determines the number of shots to be fired in each group. If a big-game rifle immediately indicates the ability to average close to minute of angle, wear and tear on its barrel and the shooter are minimized by firing three shots and allowing the barrel to cool down between each group. If a big-game rifle is capable of keeping three bullets close to or inside an inch at 100 yards, I could not care less about its five-shot accuracy. A custom Remington Model 700 in .338 Lapua I recently shot is a good example.

In contrast to that Model 700 is a recently tested 1940s-vintage Winchester 94 in .32 Special. Its first few groups at 100 yards exceeded 2 inches, so all subsequent groups fired by it contained five holes in the paper.

Varmint rifles and rifles used for competitive shooting are tested with five-shot groups. Back when I was into 3 Gun competition, some stages required emptying several AR-15 magazines. Target distances ranged from quite close to as far away as 300 yards, so when accuracy-testing a new rifle or load, 10 and sometimes 20 shots per group was the norm.

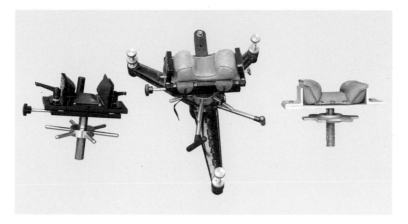

These three quick-switch tops for the Sinclair front rest handle most sizes and shapes of rifle forearms. Switching tops takes mere seconds. Levers and side pressure plates on the top allow the inside distance between the ears of the sandbag to be quickly adjusted.

The Setup

Regardless of the type of rifle or what it will be used for, I begin the program by shooting it over sandbags from a solid benchrest. The bench consists of a 4-inch-thick slab of reinforced concrete resting on concrete block pillars. It is about as steady as can be. (A small household throw rug placed atop the bench is easier on a gun's finish and the shooter's elbows than bare concrete.)

Rather than placing the chronograph atop the bench, I place it on a stool beside the one I am sitting on. Doing so makes it convenient to read, and the bench top shields it from muzzle blast.

The rifle is supported at the rear by either of two types of leather sandbags. If the shape of the cheekrest on a stock interferes with the taller ears of a rabbit-ear bag, an owl-ear bag is used. (The latter is also commonly described as a bunny-ear bag.) I have a couple of front rests and several styles of sandbags for them as well. The forearms of riflestocks vary considerably in shape and width, so a front bag matching a particular stock as closely as possible encourages consistency of hold and discourages canting of the rifle.

My Sinclair International front rest is set up with quick-switch tops holding bags of various sizes and shapes. The one I use most is called the Generation II AP Windage Top. Levers and side pressure plates allow the inside distance between the ears of its sandbag to be quickly adjusted in widths ranging in size from the narrow forearms of hunting rifles to those on varmint and target rifles measuring as wide as 3.5 inches. Switching tops takes only a bit longer than it took you to read this sentence.

Three other leather bags are used at the bench. The sausage-shaped bag measures 4 inches in diameter by 8 inches long, is filled with lead shot, and weighs 25 pounds. Used for soaking up the recoil of hard-kicking rifles, it is too thick to be placed between the shoulder and the butt of the rifle. Rather, it lies on its side with one end resting firmly against the rifle butt. Resting the stock on a rear bag positions it higher than the top of the bench, so placing the sissy bag atop a sand-filled, flat bag (called a brick bag) elevates it to the desired level. Also for comfort, I rest my right elbow on a flat sandbag called a pillow bag. The various styles of leather bags I have mentioned are shown in the Sinclair International catalog.

If the rifle will be used in the field, it is further tested by shooting over the type of rest it will likely be shot over out in the boonies. A varmint rifle wearing a Harris folding bipod is an example. If the rifle is headed to Africa, it gets shot on paper from the standing position with its forearm resting on shooting sticks. I have probably taken more of my North American game with rifles resting atop a daypack, so I make it a point to shoot a hunting rifle over one before heading for the woods. I have also taken game from the sitting position with my arm wrapped around a rifle sling in the "hasty" position. Shooting a rifle on paper the way it will likely be shot during a hunt reveals my accuracy with it in the field compared to shooting it from the bench.

Wind Flags

It is best to accuracy-test a rifle during ideal range conditions with no wind, but since Mother Nature seldom cooperates where I shoot, wind flags are used. Sometimes described as wind indicators, an entire article could be written on their design and use, but I can touch only on the high points here.

Rick Graham's Wind Flags

THROUGH THE YEARS BENCHREST SHOOTER RICK Graham has made hundreds of wind flags for his fellow competitors. His flag works exactly like the old wind vanes we used to see on the roofs of barns and houses except it relays more information to the shooter.

Sometimes described as a wind indicator, it consists of an aluminum rod with a lightweight vane at the rear and a counterweight up front. Counterweight options are a daisy wheel or a plastic ball. (I prefer the ball.) With its pivot pin supported by a Delrin bearing, the slightest breeze causes the flag to point its nose directly into it. Change in direction causes the flag to swing accordingly.

Each of the colors on a flag sends a different message to the eyes of the shooter. The ball is black at its front and white at its rear. Seeing black on the ball indicates outgoing wind. White means wind is incoming. The vane is green on one side and orange on the other. Seeing the orange side indicates wind direction is right to left. The green side toward the shooter indicates a left-to-right wind. The pink tail on the vane indicates changes in wind velocity ranging from none (tail totally limp) to very strong (tail at 90 degrees).

I learned a bit about using wind flags during my benchrest shooting days. I no longer shoot competitively, but I still find them to be useful for accuracy testing a rifle or when developing a load for one. Learning to use them takes time and patience, but once learned, those who shoot a lot will find them to be extremely useful in evaluating the accuracy of a rifle or a load.

Go to www.brflags.com for more information on Rick Graham's wind flag. Each requires a stand. I use telescoping tripods made to hold photography lights from a local camera shop, but the custom telescoping stand made by Bill Dittman (dittman@att.net) is lighter and more compact.

—Layne Simpson

Two flags placed downrange are positioned to allow me to see them in the field of view of the scope when its crosshairs are on the target. After everything is set up, I sit patiently and observe the flags long enough to spot a wind condition of fairly long duration that comes and goes more frequently than others. Then when that condition comes around, I fire my shots into the target as quickly as possible. If the flags indicate a change in condition before all the rounds of a string are fired, I stop shooting and squeeze off the remaining shots in the group only when my chosen condition returns.

The correct placement of wind flags will vary among shooting ranges, but since most of my accuracy testing is done at the same range, I know exactly where

> After everything is set up, I sit patiently and observe the flags long enough to spot a wind condition of fairly long duration that comes and goes more frequently than others.

they need to go there. Regardless of the distance, one flag is placed near the target.

One of the two Rick Graham flags I am now using has a larger vane than the other. I often shoot at 300 yards, and its size makes it easy to observe at distance. Tree lines border both sides of the private shooting range I use, and while the trees do a fairly good job of reducing wind velocity, their foliage is not dense enough to block the wind entirely. Wind is blocked even less after they shed their leaves during winter. Regardless of the time of year, the real trouble spot is a narrow gap in the left-side tree line at 215 yards. When shooting at 300 yards, the first flag is positioned in line with that opening.

Barrel Cooldowns

The barrel is cooled down completely between groups. If the cartridge a rifle is chambered for is small and heats up the barrel slowly—e.g., the .22 Hornet— several groups are fired between barrel cooldowns.

The slow way of accomplishing this is to sit and twiddle thumbs until the barrel is no longer hot. Even when testing several rifles during the same session, a lot of time is wasted while waiting, especially during the heat of summer. There are more important things in my life to be done, so a plastic bucket, a couple of plastic milk jugs full of water, and an insulated jug filled with ice cubes accompany me to the range. A rifle with a synthetic or metal stock and stainless-steel barrel can be held muzzle-down over the bucket and water poured down the outside of its barrel. This works especially well with an AR-15 wearing a handguard with openings over its entire surface.

While it should not be done with a gas-operated rifle, running water through the barrel is better because the cooling is more uniform from end to end. It is also the only way to water-cool a rifle with a wooden stock.

My homemade "barrel cooler" consists of a section of plastic tubing from the hardware store that measures 0.430 inch in diameter. It has a plastic funnel attached to one end and a cartridge case to the other. I actually have two—one with a .223 case for bores up to .35 caliber and another with a .308 case for larger calibers.

With a rifle held muzzle-down over the plastic bucket, the end of the tube is pushed into the chamber until it stops. Water is poured into the funnel slowly to avoid overflow back around the cartridge case. The barrel is immediately cooled down with absolutely no harm to it. Once the bucket becomes filled, the water is used repeatedly by dipping it out and into the funnel. Shoot enough rounds and the water will eventually become hot, at which point it is cooled down with a few ice cubes or replaced entirely with cold water. After each cooling the bore is wiped dry by pushing through three cotton patches. One fouling shot is then fired, followed by shots for record. Regardless of whether water is poured on the outside or through the bore, in no way does it harm the barrel.

Like I said, everybody has a favorite procedure for accuracy-testing rifles. And now you know about everything there is to know about mine.

Running water through a hot barrel cools it instantly with no damage. A funnel is attached to one end of the flexible plastic tubing, and a cartridge case is attached at the other. The water is caught by the bucket and reused until it becomes too hot.

Handloading For Ac

Lane Pearce reveals the accuracy secrets of his handloading mentor—secrets that have been developed over the past 45 years.

Several readers have asked how to handload the most accurate ammunition. I confess I'd never thought to write about this because the reloading manuals cover the topic thoroughly. The basic concept is simple: Make every round exactly the same as the others. Of course, as with most situations, the devil's in the details.

In my writing, I usually focus on the self-satisfaction and safety considerations associated with hand-

loading. Sometimes I remind readers that they can save money and/or shoot more for the same bucks by loading their own. However, a recent inquiry caused me to reconsider, and I'll reveal the secrets I've learned from one of my shooting mentors, John Redmon Sr., about how he achieves the best accuracy from his handloads.

First of all, Redmon is 73 years old and has probably fired a quarter of a million rounds—mostly rifle ammo—during his adult life. This

total does not include .22 rimfire because he has no idea how many cartons of those he's shot. He told me that attending college and starting a new family curtailed his hobby for several years, but since the early 1960s, he's reloaded almost every round of centerfire ammo he's fired. He started out years ago as a one-gun-does-it-all shooter. He loaded ammo for his sporterized Springfield .30-06 with heavy bullets for whitetails and light ones for ground hogs.

uracy

Lane Pearce

a handgun. "A waste of the earth's resources," is his oft-repeated assessment of shooting anything other than his favorite small-caliber rifles.

He's also quite a Remington fan. He has at least one—and sometimes two—of every Remington rimfire and centerfire rifle chambered in .22 and .24 caliber made since World War II. Notwithstanding his brusque, dry demeanor, Redmon will share his experiences with other serious shooters and handloaders. When I called him and told him what I had in mind, he readily agreed to summarize his recommendations on loading accurate ammo.

So here goes.

By taking special care in building his handloads, Lane's handloading mentor, John Redmon Sr., achieves ultimate accuracy in his small-bore rifles. Both five-shot groups shown here measure less than 0.400 inch at 100 yards (left) and 200 yards (right).

I've watched him shoot at our gun club for more than 30 years. He's even participated in some of my reloading projects but only if they involved the smaller calibers he likes to shoot. I've never seen Redmon holding a scattergun, and until just recently, I never saw him shoot

Reloading For Accuracy

As you would expect, Redmon follows a strict regimen preparing and assessing the cartridge cases. He starts with a 100-count lot of new brass, if possible, and inspects every piece for obvious defects. A fold or kink in the neck, a severely dented shoulder or case body, or a missing or off-centered flash hole relegates that piece to the scrap bucket.

Then he segregates the lot into smaller batches by weight so each

piece is within one grain. After he deburrs the flash holes and uniforms the primer pockets, he partially neck-sizes each case to round up the mouth and assure it will accept and hold the bullet securely. Finally, he trims each piece ten thousandths of an inch less than the specified maximum length and lightly deburrs the case mouths, inside and out.

He next assembles each cartridge in the separate batches with a starting charge of a medium-burn-rate propellant that is compatible with the cartridge and bullet weight he intends to load. He seats the bullets so they engrave the rifling when chambered to ensure that he obtains the proper headspace.

After fireforming the rounds in the rifle he intends to dedicate this lot of brass to, he wipes each case clean, carefully inspects it again for defects, and brushes the inside of the neck to remove any residue. He again partially resizes the necks, checks to make sure every case is less than maximum length, cleans the primer pockets, and proceeds to reload the lot.

L. P.: How about annealing, neck turning, and reaming?

J. R.: I've tried all of those processes on various occasions and concluded I was wasting my time. Of course, if you reform 7.62x51 NATO military cases into .260 Remington or .243 Winchester brass, you will have to turn or ream the necks to ensure you can load safe and reliable ammo. But it's usually a lot less trouble and expense to buy the cases you need to begin with instead of making them from another one.

L. P.: How many times can you reload a batch of cases?

J. R.: Well, about 10 to 12 times is what I've come to expect. If a neck splits, I throw the case away. If I have a rash of neck splits, I discard the whole batch and start over. I have

Redmon identifies handloads for each rifle by cartridge and serial number (last three digits). Other notations indicate load recipe, COL, date loaded, and number of times the batch has been loaded (i.e., 11 tic marks on the label on the end of the cartridge box).

annealed some brass to try to extend its usefulness, but doing it correctly is tricky, so I usually just buy more new cases.

L. P.: I've talked with a couple of competition shooters and they indicated each case has to prove it's a good one by loading and firing it several times in practice before it's used in a match. Do you track each case as to whether or not the load demonstrates satisfactory accuracy?

J. R.: I do. If I shoot a round and the bullet strikes the target out of the group, I immediately assess my technique and the prevailing conditions to determine if there was an extenuating circumstance that caused the flyer. If not, I mark the case with a felt-tip pen and segregate it from the good ones. When I load that batch again, I include the marked case and shoot it along with the good ones. If it performs okay this time, I still keep it separate, and I load and fire it once more. After another good performance, I remove the mark and return it to the general population. However, if it causes another unexplained errant bullet hole, I only reload that case for fouling shots.

L. P.: Let's talk about the energetic components. How do you select the best powder and primer?

J. R.: I shoot .222 and .223 Remington mostly now. Powder selection is arbitrary because several have

similar burn rates that may or may not work best in a specific rifle/cartridge/bullet combination. I don't pay as much attention to loading density as I do to the groups I shoot. The targets determine if I use one powder or another and how much. However, I do weigh each charge to assure the maximum uniformity of my handloads. And don't be afraid to try a different powder. I've achieved excellent results and obtained better accuracy experimenting with new propellants.

I've tried every Small Rifle primer available, and it doesn't seem to matter which one I use in proven recipes I've test-fired many times. Occasionally, it may seem like one particular handload performs better with a specific primer, but my targets don't indicate a definite trend one way or another.

L. P.: Which bullets do you prefer?

J. R.: All of the major suppliers make bullets that are good enough for loading accurate ammo. Years ago, Remington made .22- and .24-caliber benchrest bullets. I still have several thousand, and I sometimes reload a few rounds just to see if they shoot as good with today's components as they did back then. Berger's match bullets often perform much like Remington's benchrest bullets. I also like specific Sierra and

Hornady bullets in proven handloads that each rifle prefers.

L. P.: Do you segregate them like you do the brass?

J. R.: No, I don't weigh or measure each bullet. I do load each batch of handloads with a single lot of bullets to maintain uniformity.

L. P.: Do you ever swage bullets?

J. R.: A friend and I went together and bought swaging tools many years ago. We didn't make many bullets as good as we could buy, and I decided it wasn't worth the time and effort. I'd rather be shooting! Today's bullets are even better, and I can buy all I can ever load and shoot.

L. P.: Do you use coated bullets?

J. R.: I tried moly-coated bullets years ago because they promised better performance and less rifle maintenance. They didn't perform any better, and it was harder to clean my rifles if I wanted to switch back to shooting plain jacketed bullets. I don't load them anymore.

L. P.: Does seating depth affect accuracy significantly?

J. R.: Seating depth is probably the most critical factor affecting accuracy. I determine the maximum overall length for the specific bullet I intend to load the whole batch with. When I get to the range, I fire a couple of groups to assess performance. If I decide to try to achieve better results, I reseat five bullets so the overall length is ten thousandths of an inch less and shoot another group. Repeating this process, I'll find the sweet spot if it's going to be evident. Again, the targets indicate which overall length is best—or that none of them is promising, and it's time to change recipes.

L. P.: You're an engineer like me, and most engineers like lots of data. But I know you don't own a chronograph. So why don't you measure velocities to help assess the performance of your handloads?

J. R.: I have the latest reloading manuals, and after comparing the different load data, I choose new recipes to test that fall within reasonable start and maximum limits. The most recent editions provide corresponding velocities and often pressure data. So I have a good idea what my handloads are doing without measuring the velocities. I shoot at both 100 and 200 yards to determine the actual bullet trajectory and drift under varying field conditions. And, again, the targets show how close each bullet is to the others in a group. I don't need any more information to tell me if my handload is good or bad.

You and I have shot together many times. You know several factors affect accuracy—probably more so than any specific handload you happen to be testing. When I get set up at the range but don't feel calm and relaxed, I don't waste my time or ammo. I also thoroughly clean my rifles regularly to ensure I obtain the best results. Bench equipment and your shooting technique—how you support and fire the rifle—will significantly affect accuracy. Uniformity of each shot is the key to optimum accuracy.

Of course, your rifle and optics must be well-made and not impaired.

Redmon maintains meticulous shooting records of handload performance through each of his numerous Remington rifles. After shooting his home brews at the range, he files his targets and notes in the three-ring binder for that specific rifle.

For example, a marred crown or misaligned mounts will throw the bullet off or bind the scope so it can't hold a precise adjustment. How the barrel and action are bedded in the stock is very important. Trigger-pull weight and consistency are other factors that will definitely enhance or detract from how well you shoot. Chamber, throat, and bore dimensions affect how the ammo performs. You have to tailor your handloads to the specific rifle to achieve the best results.

Good handloading skills and following precise processes are extremely important in making accurate handloads. Thanks for asking me to share my experiences. I hope they will benefit from them and enjoy reloading even more.

Redmon adjusts bullet seating depth in real time at the range to determine optimum accuracy.

Achieve Maximum Accuracy from Your .22 Rimfire

Here are some ways to improve rimfire cartridge-to-cartridge uniformity in order to tighten groups.

By Layne Simpson

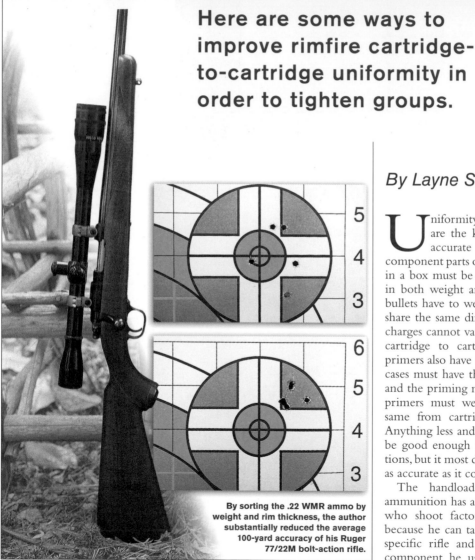

By sorting the .22 WMR ammo by weight and rim thickness, the author substantially reduced the average 100-yard accuracy of his Ruger 77/22M bolt-action rifle.

Uniformity and consistency are the keys to producing accurate ammunition. The component parts of all the cartridges in a box must be virtually identical in both weight and dimension. All bullets have to weigh the same and share the same dimensions. Powder charges cannot vary in weight from cartridge to cartridge. Cases and primers also have to be near perfect; cases must have the same capacities and the priming mix in each of the primers must weigh precisely the same from cartridge to cartridge. Anything less and the ammo might be good enough for some applications, but it most definitely won't be as accurate as it could be.

The handloader of centerfire ammunition has an edge over those who shoot factory ammo simply because he can tailor a load for his specific rifle and make sure each component he uses is as close to perfection as possible. This is why world-class benchrest shooters insist on weighing cases, spinning bullets, eyeballing primers, and performing other accuracy tricks when loading their ammunition.

None of this is possible for those who shoot .22 rimfire ammunition. And .22 rimfire ammunition is only as good as the fellow who watches the machinery that mass produces it by the millions each year decides it should be. Now don't take what I've just said in the wrong vein. Considering its affordable cost, .22 rimfire ammunition is probably better than it has a right to be, and many loads presently available are more accurate than most rifles and those who shoot them. Still, I've often wondered what I could do to make it more accurate.

Sort by Weight

Since handloading .22 rimfire ammo has yet to become practical, I began to think about how I could improve cartridge-to-cartridge uniformity. A good way to start is to make sure the boxes of cartridges bought have the same manufacturing lot number. The next step is to sort the cartridges into several groups by weight—an exercise made as easy as eating apple pie on an empty stomach by companies that sell those marvelous electronic powder scales. It doesn't matter what each individual cartridge actually weighs. But what does matter is that you end up with several groups of cartridges with every cartridge in a particular group having precisely the same weight. The cartridges stay in their respective groups—small zip-lock bags are fine for this—and are fired together.

Something else that will improve the uniformity of rimfire ammo is to improve consistency of ignition. If the firing pin of a rifle fails to

deliver consistent blows to the primers of cartridges, accuracy will suffer. Benchrest shooters who shoot the 6mm PPC and 6mm BR neck-size cases only. As a result the fit between case and chamber is so tight the case is unable to move forward as the firing pin strikes the primer. This zero headspace condition enables the firing pin to deliver the same amount of energy to each primer.

Sort by Rim Thickness

This is also why manufacturers like Anschutz who make super-accurate .22 rimfires cut special chambers in their rifles. A rimfire cartridge headspaces on its rim, and since rim thickness varies by several thousandths of an inch from cartridge to cartridge it is easy to see how resistance against the blow of the firing pin can vary from shot to shot. When the bolt is closed behind a cartridge in a match-dimension chamber, the nose of the bullet makes hard contact with the rifling and this prevents the cartridge from moving forward when struck by the firing pin, enabling the firing pin to deliver the same amount of force to each cartridge.

Since hunting rifles are subjected to a lot more dust and dirt than match rifles, the dimensions of their chambers have to be more

generous. This along with variations in the rim thickness of .22 rimfire cartridges introduces variations in firing pin energy delivery from cartridge to cartridge. In other words, since the firing pin has to push or chase a thin-rimmed cartridge some distance before it is arrested by its headspace shoulder in the chamber, the blow of the firing pin is cushioned somewhat by the free travel of the cartridge. On the other hand, since a cartridge with a thicker rim has less forward distance to travel in front of the firing pin before coming to a stop, it receives a slightly heavier blow. While the difference is not great, it is enough to introduce variations in primer mix ignition. Of course, the ideal situation would be for all cartridges to have the same rim thickness, but since this is not practical on a mass-production basis, the next best thing is to sort them by rim thickness with special gauges available from Sinclair International and Hornady Manufacturing Co.

The rim thickness gauges attach to the traveling jaw of a micrometer caliper. Dial and digital calipers are quicker to read accurately than a standard caliper, and between those two the digital has the edge in speed. The time it takes to sort through a batch of cartridges will vary from operator to operator, but I spend an average of six minutes going through 100 rounds when using a digital caliper.

To use the gauge, simply drop a cartridge into the trough of its main housing and close the jaws of the caliper. It will indicate how thick the rim of that cartridge is. The best results are obtained when the caliper is operated gently and its jaws closed on each cartridge with as much consistency in applied force as possible. I close the caliper with just the tip of my thumb and stop pushing when I feel the jaw of the caliper lightly bump against the head of the cartridge. The relatively soft

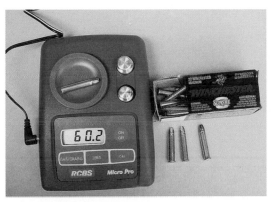
Sorting .22 WMR cartridges by weight assures better uniformity of components within individual groups of ammunition.

.22 rimfire case is quite springy and manhandling the caliper will result in false and inconsistent readings.

A long safety cord attached to the body of the gauge should be looped around one's neck as per the instructions. If the rig is dropped and strikes a solid object, a cartridge it is holding might fire; wearing the gauge in the proper manner will prevent that from happening.

Putting Four Lots of .22 WMR to the Test

I used four light-bullet loadings of the .22 WMR on varmint shoots and liked their downrange perfor-

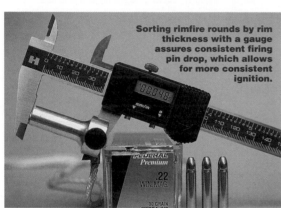

Sorting rimfire rounds by rim thickness with a gauge assures consistent firing pin drop, which allows for more consistent ignition.

mance so much that I decided to see just how accurate they could be in one of my rifles.

It became evident while sorting through the four loads that the manufacturers of .22 WMR ammunition take quality quite seriously. Among the 200 rounds of each checked for rim thickness uniformity, the Federal Premium and Winchester

Supreme loads virtually tied for first place with 67 out of each 100 Federal cartridges having exactly the same rim thickness while 66 out of each 100 Winchester cartridges measured exactly the same. Ninety-two percent of the Winchester ammo showed a rim thickness variation of no more than .001 inch; 90 percent of the Federal fodder had the same incredibly small variation. More specifically, out of each 100 rounds of Winchester ammo checked, the rims of 66 rounds measured 0.049 inch thick and 26 rounds measured 0.050 inch. As for the remaining eight rounds, six measured 0.048 inch and two measured 0.047 inch. The Federal ammo varied in rim thickness by only 0.003 inch with its percentages reading 67 at 0.046 inch, 23 at 0.047 inch, and 10 at 0.045 inch.

While the Winchester and Federal ammo held a slight edge in rim thickness uniformity, the Remington and CCI loads weren't very far behind, and they, for all practical arguments, tied for second place. Forty-eight out of each 100 rounds of the CCI ammo shared the exact same rim thickness while 41 percent of the Remington ammo measured the same. Breaking it on down a bit further, percent-

ages for the CCI fodder were 48 at 0.047 inch, 34 at 0.046 inch, 23 at 0.045 inch, and five at 0.048 inch. For the Remington ammo it was 41 at 0.044 inch, 40 at 0.043 inch, 14 at 0.042 inch, three at 0.045 inch, and two at 0.041 inch.

I sorted the four loads by weight, rim thickness, and both weight and rim thickness. To make my accuracy test results as statistically valid as possible (without spending a month at the range), I shot 40 five-shot groups with each of the four loads. Ten groups were fired with unsorted ammo; 10 groups were fired with the ammo sorted by rim thickness; 10 groups were fired with the ammo sorted by weight; and 10 groups were fired with the ammo sorted by both rim thickness and weight.

One of the test results reminded me of something I had known all along: When it comes to accuracy, some things shouldn't be taken for granted. Since an increase in cartridge rim thickness serves to tighten headspace in a .22 rimfire rifle, it is logical that the batches of ammo with thicker rims would be the most accurate. But this did not turn out to be true—at least it didn't for the test rifle.

When studying the results of my accuracy tests, keep in mind that a difference in accuracy no greater than 15 percent between the four categories is probably statistically insignificant. I arrived at this margin of error by comparing average accuracy of the first series of five five-shot groups fired with a particular load with the second series of

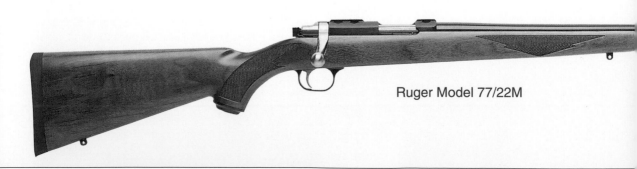

Ruger Model 77/22M

groups fired with the same ammo.

The margin of error also explains why the accuracy shown by some of the groups sorted by rim thickness or weight was actually worse than that shown for some groups of unsorted ammo. For example, the unsorted group of Federal Premium ammo proved to be more accurate than the weight-sorted group, but since the difference was only nine percent I believe we can accurately assume that separating that particular lot of that particular ammo by weight for that particular rifle had no significant effect on accuracy either way.

Statistically speaking, sorting the four loads by weight alone resulted in no significant improvement in accuracy in the test rifle in some cases. As you can see in the chart, accuracy of the "C" groups of ammo was about the same when compared to how well the unsorted "A" groups shot. On the other hand, since one of the "D" groups of ammo (sorted by both weight and rim thickness) shot almost 30 percent more accurately than the same ammo sorted by rim thickness only, it's obvious that sorting by weight most certainly is no waste of time.

Three of the "B" groups of ammo sorted by rim thickness were significantly more accurate. This indicates to me that as far as my rifle goes, this type of cartridge sorting is time well spent. In the Ruger 77/22 group sizes for Remington and Winchester improved by 64 and 52 percent. Especially significant is that in the case of the Ruger 77/22, one

rifle/ammo combination went from a two-inch average down to a 1.25-inch average while another 1.75-inch combination was squeezed down close to minute-of-angle accuracy!

Since some unsorted and sorted rifle/ammo combinations showed only minor differences in accuracy, it's obvious that nothing you have read here is carved into granite. And for that reason, I offer no guarantees.

The rifle I used obviously had plenty of accuracy potential to begin with. On the other hand, it wouldn't surprise me if some rifle/ammo combinations showed no worthwhile improvement in accuracy regardless of how much time was spent sorting the ammo. The only way to find out how well your rifle will respond is to give it a try. The very worst that can happen is you'll have lots of fun shooting your .22 rimfire.

.22 WMR Velocity/Energy Comparison

Factory Load	Velocity (fps)		Energy (ft-lbs)	
	Muzzle	100 Yards	Muzzle	100 Yards
Ruger 77/22M, 20-Inch Barrel				
CCI Maxi-Mag 30-gr. TNT	2218	1324	327	117
Federal Premium 30-gr. JHP	2277	1387	345	128
Remington Premier 33-gr. VMBT	1937	1448	275	154
Winchester Supreme 34 gr. JHP	2111	1429	336	154

NOTES. Velocity and energy figures are the average of 50 rounds.

.22 WMR Accuracy Results

Factory Load	100-Yard Accuracy (Inches)			
	(A)	(B)	(C)	(D)
Ruger 77/22M, 20-Inch Barrel, Lyman All American 20X				
CCI Maxi-Mag 30-gr. TNT	2.41	1.84*	2.52	1.72*
Federal Premium 30-gr. JHP	1.49	1.55	1.69	1.10*
Remington Premier 30-gr. VMBT	2.10	1.28*	1.97	1.35*
Winchester Supreme 34-gr. JHP	1.70	1.12*	1.52	1.21*

*With an accuracy improvement of 30 percent or greater these rifle/ammo combinations proved to be outstanding.

Ammo Category Legend
(A): Unsorted, fresh from factory box   (C): Sorted by weight
(B): Sorted by rim thickness   (D): Sorted by rim thickness and weight

NOTES: Accuracy is the average of 10 five-shot groups fired at 100 yards from a sandbag benchrest.

The Test Rifle

The rifle I used for accuracy-testing .22 WMR ammo for this report is one of my favorites. This factory-original Ruger 77/22M has been a part of my battery since soon after Ruger added that chambering to its list of options. It has a 20-inch barrel and weighs 7 1/2 pounds (with an old faithful Lyman All American 20X scope I used during the accuracy tests). Its trigger pulls 4 1/2 pounds, but its smoothness makes it feel much lighter.

Sometimes while on a prairie dog shoot I grow bored with long-range shooting with centerfire rifles. When that happens I unlimber the 77/22M for a stalk-and-shoot session. For that, Ruger's handy little .22 WMR bolt rifle is hard to beat. ∎

Why Tactical Rifles

Here's what makes tactical bolt rifles shoot those tiny long-range groups.

Tactical rifles are built to perform beyond the capabilities of the common bolt-action rifle. These long-range precision rifles have several special features.

Are So Accurate

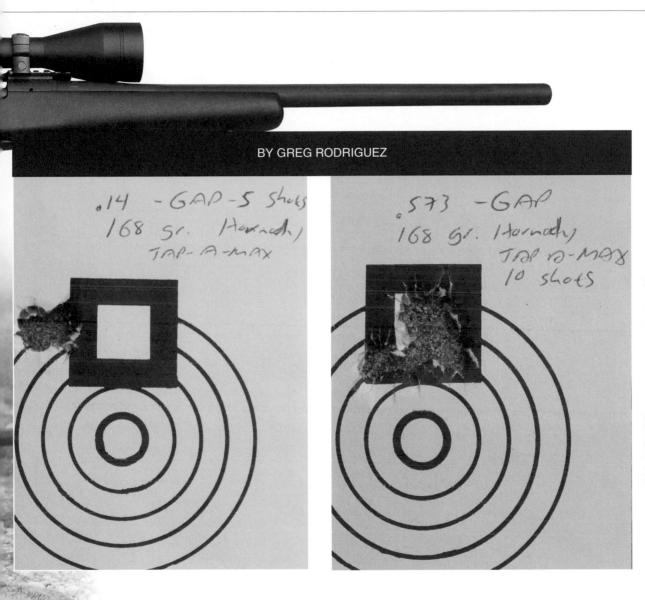

BY GREG RODRIGUEZ

.14 - GAP - 5 Shots
168 gr. Hornady
TAP - A - MAX

.573 - GAP
168 gr. Hornady
TAP A-MAX
10 shots

The rifles used by law enforcement agencies are sophisticated precision shooting instruments. They have been built to perform far beyond the capabilities of the common bolt-action rifle. While nothing can replace thousands of rounds of regular, quality practice, having the right rifle is a good place to start. I have worked with a variety of rifles at various precision rifle schools, SWAT training sessions, and rifle competitions across the country, and most tactical bolt-action rifles share several common features.

The Barrel
The barrel is the heart of a precision rifle. For the utmost accuracy, it must be stiff, heavy, and made to exacting

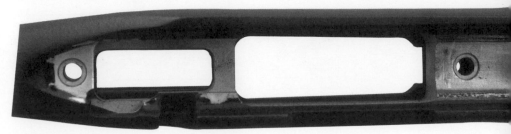

tolerances. A good barrel is smooth, with no rough spots to collect copper fouling; smooth barrels are easy to clean and can fire a lot of rounds between cleanings.

Length may vary from 20 to 24 inches, depending on the rifle's intended role. For instance, a 20-inch barrel is perfect for shooters who operate in urban environments or around vehicles, and more than adequate for shooting out to 600 or 700 yards. Although I have done a fair amount of 1000-yard work with a custom rifle with a 21-inch barrel, the higher velocities that longer barrels produce make them preferable for purposes beyond 600 yards.

Thick barrels are important on a tactical bolt-action rifle because they are stiffer and have more surface area for cooling during extended firing strings. Ideally, the barrel should have a straight taper, like the U.S. Army M24 or USMC M40 A1 rifles, rather than the more radically stepped sporter contour to ensure the utmost stiffness.

The Bedding

Bedding is simple, but it must be done properly to ensure a perfect stock-to-metal fit. This keeps the action from shifting in the stock and keeps the stock from exerting any harmonic influence on the barrel. In short, bedding eliminates a lot of the variables that can adversely affect accuracy.

For consistent, repeatable accuracy, a quality optic affixed with strong, steel mounts is a must.

There are two common types of bedding. Pillar bedding uses aluminum pillars to keep consistent pressure between the trigger guard, the action, and the stock. This also helps prevent it from crushing the stock. The addition of bedding compound keeps the receiver from shifting in the stock.

Skim bedding is also a good idea on stocks with aluminum bedding blocks. While proponents of aluminum bedding blocks may argue that bedding isn't necessary, the fact is no two stocks and actions are exactly the same, so the custom fit bedding compound provides is a great help. Another advantage of skim bedding is that it prevents side-to-side movement, while bedding blocks only prevent the action from shifting back and forth in the stock.

I once had a Remington Light Tactical rifle that shot the lights out. Unfortunately, the point of impact shifted a tiny bit each time I went to the range. I thought it was a scope problem, but my friend Matt Bettersworth of Hill Country Rifles suggested I let him bed it. The results were amazing. My point of impact didn't shift in the next three years that I owned it, and the rifle went from shooting half-inch groups to consistent, sub-quarter-inch accuracy. Aluminum bedding blocks are great, but they can still benefit from a bit of tweaking.

The Stock

The stock on a bolt-action tactical rifle must be stiff, stable, and rugged. Composite stocks of Kevlar, fiberglass, or some combination of the two are a must, not just for their ruggedness and consistency, but because they absorb a bit of recoil—a nice thing on a gun that is fired primarily from the prone position. And a good recoil pad is also a nice addition.

Because a precision rifle is fired so much from prone, the stock should have a higher comb. A high comb promotes a consistent cheek weld—a key to long-range accuracy, especially with the large objective lenses long-range shooters prefer.

A good stock will feature nice, even inletting, especially around the barrel channel, and will just "feel" right in your hands. Favorites will vary from shooter to shooter, but you'll know the perfect stock for you when you throw it to your shoulder.

The Trigger

Factory triggers are okay out of the box for general work, but precision rifles require a crisp, clean trigger. Some shooters swear by very light triggers, but three to four pounds, if it is crisp, is safer, especially when wearing gloves or under extreme stress.

Trigger jobs are relatively simple and inexpensive to perform, but they are best left to experienced gunsmiths. For shooters with especially sensitive trigger fingers or for triggers that are beyond salvation, aftermarket triggers, like those offered by Jewell or Timney, are readily available and easily installed.

The Scopes and Mounts

For consistent, repeatable accuracy, a quality optic affixed with strong, steel mounts is a must. Experienced shooters prefer one-piece bases and heavy-duty steel rings. Ideally, these should be mounted on the gun with oversized 8x40 screws.

Because many scopes do not have enough elevation adjustment to go to 1000 yards with a 100-yard zero, an angled scope base with 20 or 30 minutes of angle of elevation is essential for long-range shooting.

Several companies manufacture riflescopes specifically for tactical

bolt-action rifles. Leupold, Nikon, Schmidt & Bender, and US Optics are the brands I have used. Besides crystal-clear glass and 30mm and 34mm tubes for more erector travel and better light transmission, a tactical scope must track perfectly and offer mission-specific features such as ranging reticles, side focus, and illuminated reticles.

A Timeless Action

Precision rifles have been built on just about every action under the sun, and Remington's Model 700 dominates the bolt-action tactical rifle field. The Model 700 action is so popular because it is strong, user friendly, and consistently accurate. It's also an easy action to true for use as the base action for a custom rifle. And there are countless parts, accessories, jigs, and fixtures on the market to help get the most out of the timeless Model 700 action. Remington's tactical rifles, the Model 700 PSS and LTR, are by far the most prevalent tactical bolt-action rifles in law enforcement and civilian circles.

Although Remington's 26-inch PSS and 20-inch LTR rifles appeal to different users, both possess the qualities a precision rifle should. Both feature heavy barrels, and their barreled actions ride in H-S Precision stocks of Kevlar and fiberglass with aluminum bedding blocks. The stock on the shorter, lighter LTR is scaled down to fit its 20-inch barrel; the PSS stock is a bit thicker, with a slightly longer forend and a slight palmswell.

The barrels on both rifles feature a 5½ contour barrel that tapers quickly at first before finishing out at .840 inch at the muzzle. The 26-inch PSS barrel is smooth; the 20-inch LTR barrel has a distinctive, three-flute pattern.

A Model 700 LTR in .308 that belongs to Texas SWAT Sniper Fernando Flores, my friend and training partner, is one of the better examples to leave the Remington factory. He has not skim bedded it, but then he doesn't have to. The action fits so perfectly in the stock that his point of impact has never shifted, and it shoots ridiculously tiny groups. On a decent day his rifle will easily put five rounds of his issue Hornady ammunition into 0.25 inch.

Another training partner, Carlos Castillo, also a SWAT sniper with the same department, uses a Remington PSS. His is skim bedded, but it shot right around 0.50 inch with his duty loads before bedding. Bedding didn't improve his groups, but it has locked in his zero—he hasn't had to adjust his scope in years.

The Custom Option

Remington's factory offerings are good, but custom work is an option for those shooters looking for the utmost accuracy or those in the market for something a little different than the factory offerings.

Better barrels are the main reason most shooters go to companies like GA Precision or Hill Country Rifles for custom rifles. Broughton, Bartlein, Hart, Rock Creek, and Schneider make their barrels to more exacting tolerances than fac-

tory barrels, which shouldn't be a surprise considering that good custom barrels cost as much as some factory-produced rifles.

Custom makers are able to take more time to turn out barrels that are straighter, and they handlap them so they are smoother. Custom barrels are generally tighter and faster than factory barrels, and they can be ordered in any length and taper, with or without flutes.

Before they put on a barrel, custom makers take the time to true and square the rifle's action and lap the locking lugs, both procedures contribute to better accuracy.

Custom builders can bed a rifle in any stock, but McMillan and H-S Precision are the two most popular.

Many custom builders employ a variety of enhanced bottom metal to beef up their builds. Most choose heavy-duty parts from companies like Williams or Badger Ordnance, but some shooters opt for detachable magazine systems, such as the one from H-S Precision. I have one on a custom sniper rifle, and the flush-fit magazine gives me 10-round capacity for competitions with long shot strings.

Other popular custom features include custom, corrosion-resistant finishes; oversized recoil lugs; Harris

bipods; Eagle cheekpieces; and oversized bolt knobs.

Many of these features are simply personal preference, but some, like oversized recoil lugs, are pretty much standard modifications. In my opinion, oversized bolt knobs should be standard. The oversized knob is easier to grasp and manipulate, and its increased weight and size give the shooter improved leverage for faster, smoother bolt work without shifting position. All my precision rifles wear oversize bolt knobs.

The Ideal Rifle

Dozens of bolt-action tactical rifles have passed through my hands over the years. They varied widely in length, weight, and features. However, there is little difference between the half-dozen or so that have made it into my permanent collection. They all have precision-made barrels that are properly bedded. The stocks are stiff, stable, and rugged. The triggers have been tuned for consistent, crisp letoff. And the scopes have been carefully selected for their specific purposes. These are the features that make for a super-accurate tactical bolt action.

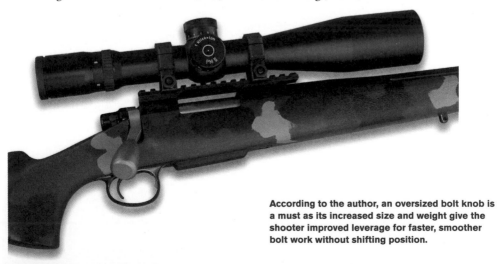

According to the author, an oversized bolt knob is a must as its increased size and weight give the shooter improved leverage for faster, smoother bolt work without shifting position.

PART II
CRITICAL PARTS
OF A RIFLE

175
GROUPS FIRED!
TWIST RATES
&
ACCURACY

BY R.L. WINDOW & DICK METCALF

There is a lot of discussion and debate these days in shooting magazines and online forums about the "best" twist rate for different styles and bullet weights of .223 Remington/5.56mm NATO cartridges, particularly for AR-platform rifles or bolt-action varmint guns. After all, "everybody knows" your rifling twist has to be right for the bullet you're shooting, and the bullet has to be appropriate for the twist. It's the conventional wisdom.

And it's no accident that the nearly congruent .223 Rem./5.56mm NATO duo is front and center in these debates. For one thing, the .223 Rem. is the largest volume consumer-selling centerfire rifle cartridge in existence. Everybody uses it.

For another, today's AR rifle manufacturers take great pains to make their customers aware of twist-rate options because it is well known that the original "mismatch" of twist rate to 5.56mm bullet weight in first-generation M16 rifles almost doomed the AR platform from the outset. The first M16 rifles built by Colt in the mid-1960s had barrels with a 1:14 twist rate. That was fast enough to stabilize standard mil-spec 55-grain FMJ bullets at "normal" ambient temperatures, but bullets became unstable below 32 degrees Fahrenheit. That prompted the Army to switch to a slightly faster 1:12 twist, and then later when the 62-grain SS109/M855 bullet was adopted, the specified twist became a much faster 1:7.

Plus, the range of bullet weights for .223/5.56mm cartridges is extremely wide, with nearly a 300 percent difference between the lightest and heaviest that are commercially available, making them much more susceptible to twist-rate effects at the outer limits than bigger-bore cartridges that are offered within a much narrower range of bullet weights and styles.

So, everybody knows having the "correct" twist rate is important. Everybody knows long, heavy bullets require a fast twist rate to stabilize properly. Everybody knows slow twist rates are really appropriate only for lighter, shorter bullets. And everybody knows using a twist rate that is mismatched to the bullet makes a difference in accuracy.

But how much difference?

If you're buying a .223/5.56mm AR-15 as a "general-purpose rifle" for common and popular commercial ammunition, what difference does it really make whether it has a 1:7, a 1:8, or a 1:9 twist? Can a mere 1-inch difference in twist rate really make that much difference in performance with popular bullets that only differ in weight by a few grains—like 55 or 60? If you're buying a varmint rifle with a typical 1:12 twist, what is the heaviest bullet load you can use before the slower twist will have a negative effect on accuracy? How can you find out? Before going there, let's first look a little closer at the kindergarten basics.

The Spin on Twist

Rifling spins a bullet to stabilize its flight. Twist rates are expressed as the number of inches the bullet travels down the barrel for one complete rotation of the

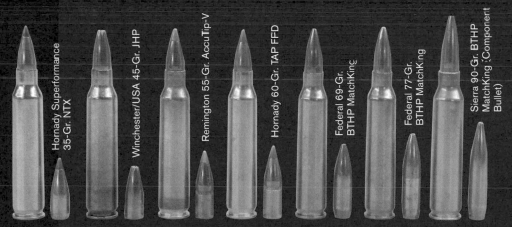

Cartridges and bullet weights used in this report demonstrate the interesting aspects of bullet weight to length ratio. The lightweight 35-grain GMX is bigger than the 45-grain JHP because of its nonlead composition.

The two vastly different .223 rifles with 1:7-twist rates both shot best with heavy-bullet match loads.

Savage Model 12 VLP DBM With Federal 77-Gr. BTHP

Colt AR-15/M4 With Federal 69-Gr. BTHP

bullet. A 1:10 twist indicates one rotation per 10 inches of travel. As a general rule, the greater a bullet's overall length, the faster the twist required to stabilize it. That last sentence is important because it didn't say "weight." It said "length." Most people discuss twist-rate effects solely in terms of whether bullets are heavier or lighter. That misses a crucial point. Yes, longer bullets do tend to be heavier than shorter bullets, but only if they are of similar construction. A heavy lead-core bullet may in fact be notably shorter than a lighter all-copper bullet. The stabilizing effect of any rate of twist

on any bullet is a complex interaction involving its individual mass, specific gravity, length, velocity, and overall shape. You cannot tie the effect of twist solely to bullet weight alone.

Plus, bullets for all centerfire rifle calibers are available in a variety of lengths and weights, both as hand-loading components and in commercial ammunition, so production-manufactured rifles generally employ a "standard" twist rate that will stabilize the majority of bullets generally used in those rifles' cartridges. These standards are set by organizations, such as the Small

Arms and Ammunition Manufacturers' Institute (SAAMI), and provide a common ground all barrel manufacturers and their customers can depend on. This approach works in general because a shorter, lighter bullet will stabilize even if "overspun" faster than absolutely necessary. It is only when a bullet is longer than a given twist can handle that stability becomes an issue. Bullets that are not stable will yaw in flight and will lose accuracy. In extreme cases the bullets may tumble and will "keyhole" on target instead of producing round holes, if they hit the target at all. By and large, it's

The Remington R-15 Varmint (top) with 1:9 twist shot best with Remington's 55-grain AccuTip load, whereas the DPMS Prairie Panther (bottom) with 1:8 twist was most accurate with Winchester's USA 45-grain JHP load. Both bullets fall into the mid-to-light weight range.

Rifle Mfg. Model Barrel Length (Inches) Twist Rate Bullet Weight	Colt M4 Sporter 16 1:7 Accuracy (Inches)	Savage 12 VLP DBM 26 1:7 Accuracy (Inches)	DPMS Prairie Panther 20 1:8 Accuracy (Inches)	Remington R-15 Varmint 24 1:9 Accuracy (Inches)	T/C Encore 24 1:12 Accuracy (Inches)	Average Accuracy Per Load (Inches)
35-Gr. Hornady NTX Superformance, BC: .109	1.917	0.708	1.770	0.875	1.396	1.333
45-Gr. Winchester/USA JHP, BC: .198	2.312	0.687	0.687	0.843	0.583	1.022
55-Gr. Remington AccuTip-V, BC: .255	1.583	1.208	2.229	0.562	1.333	1.383
60-Gr. Hornady TAP FPD, BC: .265	1.437	0.812	1.032	0.750	0.792	0.965
69-Gr. Federal BTHP MatchKing, BC: .305	0.750	1.166	1.750	0.641	1.437	1.149
77-Gr. Federal BTHP MatchKing, BC: .362	1.437	0.583	1.750	1.000	5.583	2.071
90-Gr. Sierra BTHP MatchKing (handload*), BC: .511	1.417	0.729	2.542	6.458	26.312	7.492
Average Accuracy Per Rifle (Inches)	1.550	0.842	1.680	1.590	5.348	
Average Accuracy for All Groups (Inches)	2.202					

* The handload consisted of 24.0 grains of H414.

better to overspin a shorter/lighter bullet than to underspin a longer/heavier bullet.

It is also important to understand that the "standard" twist rate for any given cartridge is calculated to be the best all-round rate for that cartridge overall, not to be the best twist rate for any particular bullet. The only way to get optimum performance for a particular bullet in any cartridge is to use a barrel with the best twist rate available for that specific bullet. So if you want a rifle to use with a variety of different loads, you'll just have to accept the fact that you'll be functioning at a lowest common denominator level. The only way to get the best that gun can do is to shoot it only with a bullet to which its bore is truly married.

Bullets that are longer than average usually have higher ballistic coefficients and are designed for long-range shooting. Like lead-free bullets that are longer than conventional bullets for a given weight, these bullets may only stabilize in specifically designed faster-twist barrels. Component bullet manufacturers recommend specific twist rates for their specific products, which also apply to commercial ammo using those bullets. Same-caliber bullets having close or congruent ballistic coefficients also generally fly well from the same twist rates.

In order to make the best use of all that information, you need to know the twist rate of the barrel in which you will be firing those bullets. How can you find out your particular rifle's twist rate? Today,

The Thompson/Center Encore with 24-Inch, 1:12-twist barrel shot best with economy-priced 45-grain Winchester/USA prairie dog loads.

many manufacturers stamp the twist rate on the barrel itself, particularly if it is a "nonstandard" rate. Or you can find twist-rate information in many firearm manufacturers' catalogs. And you can easily determine your barrel's twist rate yourself. To measure the twist rate of a barrel, simply use a cleaning rod with a closely fitted patch that will cause the rod to rotate with the rifling as you push it through the bore. Mark the rod so you can see when it makes one complete revolution, then measure how far you have pushed the rod into the barrel at that point. This will tell you how far the bullet has to go through your barrel to make one full revolution.

Measuring Twist Effects

With all that said, the basic questions remain. Today's long list of factory-built .223 rifles are available with rifling twist rates running from 1:7 to 1:12. Commercial .223 Rem. ammunition is widely available in bullet weights running from 35 grains to 80+ grains (with major-brand bullets up to 90 grains available for handloading). Rifles chambered for .223 with 1:9-twist rifling are widely perceived as the best all-round "compromise" choice for general use with the widest range of ammo. But are they? How much actual difference on-target

will using the "wrong" .223 bullet in your particular-twist .223 rifle actually make? Is there in fact a repeatable, dependable correlation between progressively faster/slower twist rates and progressively heavier/lighter bullets that can be depended upon as a guide to making individual rifle and ammo purchase choices? *Shooting Times* decided to try to find out and to see if we could cast a little more light on the entire issue of twist-rate/bullet-weight effects.

For ammunition we selected six popular .223 commercial loads plus one handload, running in bullet weights (and progressively higher ballistic coefficients) at roughly 10-grain intervals from 35 to 90 grains. The list included: 35-grain Hornady NTX Superformance (a nontoxic, nonlead bullet), 45-grain Winchester/USA JHP (a very cost-effective varmint shooter's load), 55-grain Remington AccuTip-V (preferred by many high-end coyote hunters), 60-grain Hornady TAP FPD (a dedicated law enforcement and defense load), 69-grain Federal BTHP MatchKing (a popular competition load), 77-grain Federal BTHP MatchKing (a heavy-bullet competition load), and 90-grain Sierra BTHP MatchKing handload (an extreme long-range competition load, sized for hand feeding into the chambers).

Our selection of .223 rifles included the four different twist rates currently offered in factory production as follows: 1:7-twist Colt M4 Model SP6920 with 16.1-inch barrel, 1:7-twist Savage Model 12 F/TR with 30-inch barrel, 1:8-twist DPMS Prairie Panther with 20-inch barrel, 1:9-twist Remington R-15 Varmint with 24-inch barrel, and 1:12-twist T/C Encore Rifle with 24-inch barrel. We used two separate 1:7-twist rifles because of the extreme disparity of their formats, one being a military-format AR carbine with the current mil-spec twist, the other a 30-inch precision match bolt-action rifle specced for heavy-bullet competition. They were the longest and the shortest barrels available, and we figured it would be interesting to see if their common twist rate might overshadow their obvious differences.

We would have liked to have used even more different twists, and more were formerly available. The original M16, which initiated the furor against the AR-15 platform as inaccurate, had a 1:14-twist barrel. It was quickly abandoned, and a 1:14 twist is no longer to be found on any production .223 gun. There were also formerly several .223 sporting rifles available with 1:10-twist bores; again, that one is no longer offered. Apparently, the 1:12 twist has replaced the 1:10 entirely as far as sporting .223 rifles are concerned. On the very fast-twist side, Sierra Bullets recommends a minimum 1:6.5 twist for handloading its 90-grain MatchKing BTHP, but 1:6.5 barrels for the .223 Rem. are available only from two custom barrel makers that I could find, and then only with extremely long waiting periods. Bottom line: For factory-production .223 rifles today, 1:7, 1:8, 1:9, and 1:12 twists are it.

Handloads with the Sierra 90-grain MatchKing were all sized to the same overall length regardless of the rifle to ensure consistency of the results.

CAUTION
All load data should be used with caution. Always start with reduced loads first and make sure they are safe in each of your guns before proceeding to the high test loads listed. Since *Shooting Times* has no control over your choice of components, guns, or actual loadings, neither *Shooting Times* nor the various firearms and components manufacturers assume any responsibility for the use of this data.

The test protocol was simple. We fired five, three-round groups with each of the seven selected loads through each of the five rifles at 100 yards, for a total of 175 groups. The average group results were plotted on the accompanying chart, with bullets by ascending weight on the vertical axis and bores by twist rate (fast to slow) on the horizontal axis. In examining the chart, it is important to understand that no comparison of these guns' absolute accuracy is intended or implied ("rating" a 16-inch AR tactical carbine against a 30-inch F-Class match rifle would be pretty silly, after all). What is being demonstrated is the relative accuracy of each different bullet-weight load with each different rate of rifling twist. And from that perspective, the results are very interesting.

Comparing the Results

Comparing overall group averages by rifling twist rate, it is immediately apparent that the conventional wisdom about the 1:9 twist being the best overall compromise holds generally true, providing sub-MOA results with all bullets in the popular midweight .223 load categories. Also, the best individual averages for the heaviest weight, highest ballistic coefficient bullets tend to fall into the lower left-hand quadrant of the chart, which is where they should if the heavy-bullet/fast-twist rule holds. Similarly, the overall best averages for the lightest weight bullets pattern in the upper right-hand quadrant. The overall worst averages are in the lower right-hand corner, where the heaviest bullets encoun-

The best single 100-yard group fired during the review series measured 0.437 inch and came with the 55-grain AccuTip loading and the Remington R-15 Varmint rifle with 1:9 twist.

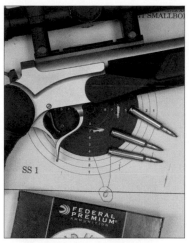

Bullets heavier than 70 grains simply will not stabilize in slow 1:12-twist rifles. They tend to print perfect keyholes on 100-yard targets.

tered the slowest twists and printed erratic keyhole patterns.

But what is really interesting is how widely the results with individual loads in individual guns diverged from the conventionally accepted rule of thumb. The best average for the heavy Federal 69-grain Match load came from the 1:9-twist bore, not from the 1:7- or 1:8-twist bores. The 1:9 bore also delivered the best 55-grain accuracy. The light Winchester/USA 45-grain JHP shot best from the 1:12-twist T/C varmint bore, but averaged only 0.1 inch better there than it did from the 1:8-twist or the 1:7-twist Savage bolt action. That Savage match rifle was of course the wild card, but I'm glad I included it because its overall performance clearly demonstrates how characteristics, features, and quality in an individual rifle can reduce other variables, such as rifling twist, to near-insignificance. It shot sub-MOA from lightest to heaviest and was the only gun to do so.

The bottom line is that conventional wisdom about the relationship between twist rate and bullet weight/length does generally hold true, but only in general, and not as applies to individual loads in individual bores. For each individual rifle, with any individual load, all bets are off, and there's simply no predicting which bullet weight will shoot best in which rifle with which twist rate. Who would have expected that the best individual average recorded in this entire protocol would have come from the 55-grain load through the 1:9-twist barrel? Who would have expected the Hornady 60-grain TAP FPD load to be the only bullet to record an overall sub-MOA average for all groups fired through all five different-twist barrels?

Conventional wisdom and rules of thumb are fine, but the only way to really find out what bullets shoot best in your gun is just to take it out and shoot it—with everything.

Lapping a Rifle Barrel

REID COFFIELD

If someone suggested you rub the inside of your rifle barrel with sand, would you do it? That's a pretty stupid question, right? Of course you wouldn't.

From day one, we're taught to treat the bore with TLC. We're admonished by every gun expert, self-proclaimed and otherwise, to be extra careful and never allow the slightest amount of wear or smallest bit of abrasive to make even the tiniest scratch inside the barrel.

The rifle bore is one of those mysterious and sacred areas we can only approach with care and by following the specific instructions of experts. After all, if we do anything wrong, we'll ruin the barrel, or so we're told. But like so much popular wisdom, that's not always true.

Over the years, I've developed an interest in older military bolt-action rifles. One of the things I've discovered is if I can afford the rifle, it's probably not in the best shape. In fact, it's pretty safe to say it'll be darn rough! That's okay with me; I'd much rather have a rifle that saw use than a mint-condition example that was never issued.

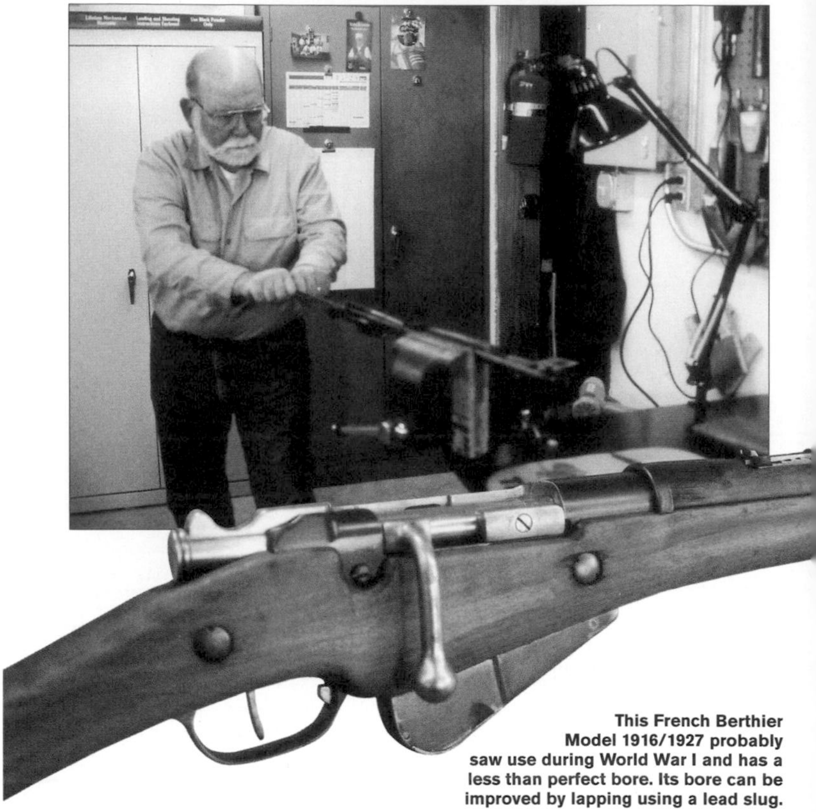

The problem with these old rifles is compounded by the fact that most military ammo used up through the end of World War II had corrosive primers. If you're standing in mud with somebody shooting at you, you seldom have the time or inclination to go through all the machinations necessary to thoroughly clean your rifle after firing corrosive ammo. Consequently, many—if not most—of these old warhorses have pretty rough bores with pitting ranging

This French Berthier Model 1916/1927 probably saw use during World War I and has a less than perfect bore. Its bore can be improved by lapping using a lead slug.

from light to "oh my gosh."

If I just wanted to hang these old rifles on the wall, the bore condition wouldn't matter all that much. But for me, part of the romance of these rifles is taking them to the range and firing them. It's one thing to read about 'em, but I want to know what it feels like, how it sounds, and even its aroma after firing.

The problems with a rough bore are that it hurts accuracy and leads to excessive fouling. The pits actually rip metal from the bullet as it passes down the bore. If nothing

else, this roughness makes cleaning a real chore.

One way to deal with a bad barrel is to smooth the bore and remove, or at least lessen, the effects of the pitting. That's were the sand comes in.

The only way to smooth the bore is to go over it with an abrasive such as silicone carbide, which is basically like super-fine sand. There are two ways of getting the abrasive into the bore. The quickest is to coat a bullet with abrasive and fire it through the bore. This is called fire lapping and has become quite popular in the last few years. The other method, which I prefer, is a more traditional lapping technique using a lead slug, abrasive, and a sturdy rod. Now keep in mind that I'm talking about rifles with barrels just one step away from being used as tomato stakes. I'm not talking about super-nice commercial barrels or wringing sub-minute-of-angle accuracy from them. If you've got a barrel like that, go see a good gunsmith. I'm dealing with ratty old barrels, and any improvement I make is a net gain.

Traditional lead lapping of a barrel begins by disassembling the rifle and thoroughly cleaning the bore. Spend as much time as necessary to remove any carbon or bullet-jacket fouling. After an extensive cleaning, you may be surprised to find the bore actually looks worse and even rougher! In cleaning, you may have emptied the pits of built-up fouling, and the bore appears to be worse. That has happened to me on a number of occasions.

With the bore cleaned, take a sturdy cleaning rod with a jag or metal patch loop and insert it from the breech end until the jag or loop and a half-inch or so of the rod

Coffield uses a hot air gun to heat the barrel prior to casting the lap in the bore.

projects from the muzzle. Take a bit of regular cotton twine and wrap it around the rod just ahead of the muzzle. Use enough twine to form a good seal around the rod. This will prevent the liquid lead we use to form the lap from flowing past the twine seal and into the barrel.

Use a hot air gun or propane torch to heat the barrel from the muzzle back about 3 or 4 inches or so. The barrel doesn't have to be super hot, just very warm to the touch. A heated barrel will minimize voids or imperfec-

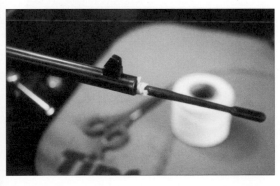

Cotton twine is wrapped around the rod to seal the bore under the lead lap.

tions in the lead casting. It's also a good idea to heat the jag or loop.

When you have it properly heated, pull the rod back into the barrel until the top of the loop is about one inch below the muzzle. Pour in melted lead until the lead is even with the muzzle. Needless to say, be darn careful and wear gloves and protective clothing. Hot, molten lead can cause severe burns. That's also another good reason to have the barreled action out of the stock and supported in a padded vise.

By the way, I use almost pure lead because it's softer than lead with a high tin or antimony content. The pure-lead lap moves through the bore much easier than a hard lead alloy lap.

Allow a few minutes for the lead lap to cool and solidify. Next, push the rod from the breech so the lap extends forward out of the muzzle about 3 inches. I use a 6-inch coarse flat file to remove any lead extending out further than the diameter of the bore. More often than not there's a "button" of lead that extends into the crown. If you don't file it away, you'll never be able to pull the lap through the barrel.

Use a small file to cut some grooves around the lap. This can be one long spiral groove or several separate circular grooves; it really doesn't matter. The important thing is that you have these grooves to help carry some of the lapping abrasive.

While you could use almost any abrasive, with these old barrels I have found that Clover silicone carbide grease-based abrasive—

The molten lead is carefully poured into the muzzle end of the barrel.

Note the lead "button" that has formed as the lead spreads out into the crown of the muzzle. The flange of the "button" must be removed before the lap can be pulled into the bore.

lap out of the barrel, just melt the lap off the rod and start over. A piece of tape wrapped around the rod about 4 inches below the lap is a good, simple means of keeping track of the location of the lap as it nears the chamber.

Pulling the lap through the barrel can be very tough initially, especially if the bore is rough. As you work the lap back and forth in the barrel, it will begin to move more easily. After about a dozen strokes or so, you'll feel a noticeable difference. This is due to wear on the lap and the abrasive smoothing the bore.

As the lap wears, you'll want to melt off the old one and recast a new, tight lap. I use my hot air gun to do this, but you can also use a propane torch. I generally replace the lap three or four times while using the same grit of abrasive. Once I have completed a series of three or four laps with the initial 120-

generally available in automotive parts stores—works just fine. I have a shop sampler kit with 2-ounce tins in grits from 120 up to 800. I seldom need to use finer than the 240 grit.

I apply the grit by simply putting a bit on my finger and rubbing it over the lap. It doesn't take much. In fact, if you use too much, it'll make pulling the lap through the bore almost impossible.

With the lap loaded with abrasive, the cleaning rod is pulled back through the bore. By the way, I use an old cleaning rod designed for use with the M14 rifle. Be very careful that you don't pull the rod so far that the lap disengages from the rifling. If you accidentally pull the

grit abrasive, I clean the barrel and check my work. I generally notice a significant difference in how easily a cleaning patch will move through the bore. There is also a visual difference in the brightness of the bore. It just looks better!

Coffield prefers almost pure lead for barrel lapping.

A simple Lee melting pot is ideal for preparing the lead.

Depending upon the condition of the bore, I repeat this cycle of steps with 180- and then 240-grit abrasive. Each time, the bore should look and feel smoother. Just how far you should go with higher grit abrasives or how long you should lap the barrel is entirely subjective. Do it until you're satisfied. If you later decide you want the bore smoother, just pull out the lapping supplies and go for it.

Lapping old military rifles will not make a rusty tube into a prize-winning match barrel, but it can help to make the rifle more enjoyable to shoot. It's just amazing what you can do with a little bit of sand.

Until next time, good luck and good gunsmithing!

Clover lapping compound is a grease-based silicone carbide abrasive available at many auto parts stores.

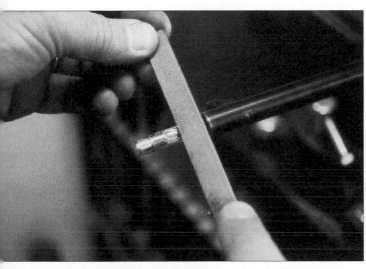

small, coarse, flat file is used to cut grooves around the lap (top), and the abrasive paste is applied sparingly to the lap (bottom).

Make sure you have a very sturdy rod for the lap. Coffield uses an old surplus M14 steel cleaning rod.

MUZZLE CROWN:

THE ALL-IMPORTANT END

By Richard Mann

Every accuracy addict knows that a small problem at the muzzle translates into a big problem downrange. But there's a simple solution.

As a bullet leaves a rifle's barrel on the way to its intended destination, its last contact is with the crown of the muzzle. As the bullet departs, gases escape between the base of the bullet and the face of the muzzle. The concentricity of the bullet's base and the crown on the muzzle and the relationship between these two allow the gases to escape evenly. The premise is that this prevents the bullet's flight from being disturbed, allowing you to knock that tick off a hound dog as Daniel Boone bragged his rifle would do.

Take a water hose without a nozzle and turn the water on full force. Then stick your thumb over the edge of the end of the hose so that it just touches the stream of water. Notice how this changes the characteristics of the spray. This sort of illustrates how a small deformity in the crown of a rifle barrel can affect exiting gas as the bullet leaves the barrel. With the water hose you are dealing with pressures of about 40 psi; with a rifle they are substantially higher, and even small deformities have influence. And, as any accuracy addict knows, a little problem at the muzzle translates into a big problem downrange.

There are various theories about what constitutes a proper muzzle crown. No doubt you have heard about an 11-degree target crown that some benchrest shooters regard as the Holy Grail of muzzle ends. But what all generally agree on is that a crown in conjunction with the face of the muzzle should do two things: protect the end of or edge of the rifling from damage and provide a geometrically consistent and even hole in the end of the barrel as it relates to bullet exit.

The face of a barrel and muzzle crown are two different things. When a muzzle is faced it can be cut flat (at a 90-degree angle), or it can be concave (recessed). The muzzle face references the end of the barrel; the muzzle crown describes the treatment of the end of the lands and grooves in the rifle's bore. For the crown to work properly, it and the face of the muzzle must be applied at a 90-degree angle to the centerline of the bore, which is not the same thing as 90 degrees to the outside geometry of the barrel because all barrels have some degree of "run-out" meaning the hole is not exactly in the center.

Finding more enjoyment in exploratory experiments with firearms than I do watching reality TV, I decided to conduct some tests. Few of us have the funds or resources to go cutting on, and/or tampering with, our rifles just to discover if certain things work. Luckily, when I told a gunsmith friend what I wanted to do, he offered up several rifles that he purchased only for their actions. So with volunteer rifles donated I began some muzzle crown experimentation.

The first two rifles were .30-06: a Remington Model 700 and a Winchester Model 70. Both were fired with Winchester 180-grain Power-Point factory loads to establish their accuracy potential. That done, I took a chisel and, though it somewhat made my knees weak, pinged a divot on the crown of each barrel at about seven o'clock. This damage is

Muzzle Crowning Techniques

Most factory rifle barrels are faced and crowned in the same operation. Custom builders perform the operation in several steps in a fashion they consider either magical or socially acceptable. Charlie Sisk at Sisk Rifles applies an 11-degree crown using piloted crowning tools, but Melvin Forbes at New Ultra Light Arms has a different approach. New Ultra Light Arms rifles have a reputation for accuracy even though they are some of the lightest rifles made. There are a number of reasons for this and being properly crowned is surely one of them. Forbes uses ball-shaped cutters called "carbide burrs" to crown barrels by hand after they have been given a radiused face for protection. The logic is simple, piloted crowning tools rely on the pilot to find the center of the bore, but for a pilot to go inside the bore it must be smaller than the bore, which means it does not fit "perfectly." With the ball cutter, the ball naturally finds the center of the bore.

Forbes only uses three ball sizes for every caliber rifle he makes. This means that the angle of the crown on a .223 barrel will be different than on a .243 barrel because the same cutter is used for both, and it will slip deeper into the bore of the .243-caliber barrel. I know of no one else using the "Forbes" method, but that's nothing new, Forbes does a number of things to rifles that no one else does.

Dave Kiff at Pacific Tool & Gauge supplies rifle builders, factory and custom, with cutting tools, and he suggests an 11-degree crown. (Actually, this is a 79-degree crown when considered in relation to the axis of the bore. The reamer is cut on an 11-degree angle.) But Kiff also suggests kissing the 11-degree crown with a 60-degree bevel. His reasoning is that the sharp, 79-degree cut with the 11-degree reamer will leave a burr on the inside edge of the bore much like you see when you sharpen a knife blade and have that "rolled" edge. Kiff tells me he sells quite a few 11-degree crowning reamers along with the 60-degree taper tool to benchrest shooters who are screaming the praises of this combination. ∎

To prove how recrowning can improve a rifle's accuracy, the author conducted accuracy tests with untouched factory crowns and crowns that he resurfaced. In each case the effect on accuracy was significant.

Winchester Model 70

Muzzle Crown Tests
100-Yard Accuracy (Inches)

Crown Condition	.30-06 Winchester Model 70				.30-06 Remington Model 700			
	Group 1	Group 2	Group 3	Average	Group 1	Group 2	Group 3	Average
Factory (untouched)	2.13	0.37	1.29	1.26	2.23	2.91	1.55	2.23
Damaged	1.15	2.88	3.38	2.47	1.64	1.61	1.17	1.47
Recrowned	1.03	0.59	1.41	1.01	1.23	1.10	0.42	0.91

NOTES: Accuracy is for five-shot groups fired from a sandbag benchrest at 100 yards. A Manson tool was used for recrowning the Winchester Model 70, and a Brownells tool was used for recrowning the Remington Model 700.

more severe than might be obtained during normal use, but I wanted to exaggerate the effect. Accuracy was then tested with each injured crown, and two things happened that surprised me. First, the average group size for the Remington Model 700 shrank from 2.23 inches to 1.47 inches. Second, the point of impact for both rifles rose over five inches!

Somewhat perplexed with the results, I recrowned both barrels using two different crowning tools. This took about the same amount of time that was required to fire the test groups with each rifle. Back on the bench both rifles not only shot better than they did with the damaged crown, but they shot better than with the factory crown. One might also recognize that after the recrowning by a run-of-the-mill hillbilly such as myself, both rifles shot pretty doggone well using factory ammunition. I know gents who carry groups this size around in their wallets for show-and-tell along the counter at a friend's gunshop.

For another test I took a Weatherby Vanguard in .300 Winchester Magnum and fired three three-shot groups with four different factory loads to establish a base accuracy. Taking an 11-degree crowning tool supplied by Pacific Tool & Gauge, I then touched up the barrel's crown. This actually entailed refacing the muzzle in order to get the 11-degree cutter deep enough to engage the ends of the lands and grooves because the Weatherby's muzzle was radiused from the factory. This refacing was accomplished with a tool from Manson Reamers. Then three more three-shot groups were fired with each load. Finally, I kissed the 11-degree crown with a 60-degree tool and went back to the shooting bench.

Two things became very apparent. First, the Caldwell Lead Sled may be the best invention since Excedrin. Go ahead, call me a wimp, but by the time I got to the last 36-round volley I dreaded each trigger pull like a visit to the dentist. And that was even with using the Lead Sled. I don't even want to think about what all that

11 Degree Muzzle Crown Tests

100-Yard Accuracy (Inches)

Factory Load	Crown Type		
	Factory (Untouched)	11 Degree	11 Degree With 60 Degree Finish
.300 Winchester Magnum Weatherby Vanguard			
Winchester 150-gr. XP^3	2.29	1.96	1.55
Federal High Energy 180-gr. Trophy Bonded	1.53	1.37	1.60
Nosler Custom 180-gr. Partition	1.22	1.30	0.90
Winchester 180-gr. XP^3	1.51	1.30	1.50

NOTES: Accuracy is the average of three three-shot groups fired from a sandbag benchrest at 100 yards.

shooting would have felt like without the Lead Sled. Second, both the Winchester 150-grain XP3 load and Nosler's Custom Ammunition load using 180-grain Partitions showed substantial improvement. Flyers in the final groups with the other two loads increased their average and may have been a result of shooter fatigue. (I have no intention of repeating the experiment!) In any case, the results seem to support the idea that an 11-degree crown finished off with a 60-degree bevel works—at least in this isolated example.

I asked Melvin Forbes at New Ultra Light Arms what he thought about my crowning achievement, and he thought that in this case the initial facing and 11-degree taper was likely more precise than the factory crown and provided a good face to the end of the barrel, allowing the 60-degree tool to cut a bevel that was smooth and centered. He added that when that can be achieved the actual angle of the crown was immaterial to accuracy.

Bottom line, I have learned that a touch up of a barrel's crown might save countless hours at the loading bench and may very well enhance the accuracy potential of a brand-new factory rifle or an old clunker. Crowning tools are not that expensive when you consider the time and money load development or a rebarreling job can consume.

Muzzle Crowning Tools

Manson Muzzle Crown Re-Facing Tool Kit: This kit is manufactured by Dave Manson Precision Reamers and is available direct from Manson or from Brownells. It is practically idiotproof and can be purchased with from two to 10 pilots that are fixed in the bore by tension. The cutter rotates on the pilot. Eleven- and zero-degree cutters are supplied.

Brownells Rifle/Handgun Muzzle & Cylinder Facing And Chamfering Tools: These tools utilize interchangeable fixed pilots and are available as a 90-degree facing tool and a 45-degree chamfering/crowning tool. They are uncomplicated and easy to use.

Pacific Tool & Gauge Facing And Crowning Reamers: Sixty-degree center reamers and 79-degree (11-degree) crown reamers are ready to be delivered, but Pacific can make a custom reamer to your specifications. These reamers have rotating pilots that can be changed to fit a specific bore size. You will need a standard die and tap handle, which can be picked up at most any quality hardware store.

Carbide Burrs: This is the tool used by Melvin Forbes for crowning barrels at New Ultra Light Arms. These tools are available from most metalworking suppliers like J&L Industrial Supply. You will need some mechanism or handle to attach to the cutter.

Brownells 45-Degree Tool

Brownells 90-Degree Tool

The Most Important Part of a Rifle

BY RICHARD MANN

When it comes to achieving optimum accuracy, a good trigger is paramount.

The trigger may be the most important mechanical part of a rifle, so it deserves attention. It is the "go" switch, and if you are looking to place bullets accurately, you will need a trigger that operates at the highest level of precision.

When a shooter squeezes a trigger, a series of events is set in motion that hopefully results in the bullet striking the intended spot. For this to happen the shooter must properly manipulate the trigger, and the trigger must release without disturbing the relationship of the rifle to the point of aim. Other variables, such as sights and the interaction between the rifle and ammunition, also influence accuracy, but to

realize the full potential of a rifle we should do our part to eliminate the influences that trigger function have in the equation. This means we must learn to squeeze triggers and make sure the triggers provide consistent operation. A trigger that breaks crisply and cleanly with minimal take-up, creep, and overtravel is much easier to master.

How Triggers Work

When a trigger is pressed the trigger or a trigger bar that is

Tight groups are impossible to attain with a trigger that demonstrates long take-up, creep, or overtravel. Using a good, consistent trigger allows a rifle to perform to its potential.

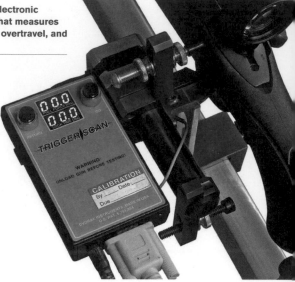

The Dvorak TriggerScan is an electronic trigger-pull measuring device that measures and records pull weight, creep, overtravel, and locktime.

connected to the trigger releases the sear, which is under spring tension. The sear then falls away from the cocking piece or hammer, which in turn makes the firing pin strike the primer. A rough bearing surface between the trigger and sear will feel gritty and will release at an unpre-dictable moment. Too much bearing surface will result in excessive creep, but not enough bearing surface can be dangerous. Last year a professional hunter in Africa was showing me his new "stopping rifle" in .458 Lott. The trigger had been "worked" and on occasion when the rifle's safety was placed to "Fire," the rifle would go bang! The first time this happened he launched a 500-grain solid over the mountain behind his lodge. The culprit was insufficient sear engagement. The trigger pull was light and crisp but extremely dangerous; a few stokes with a flat file "safed-up" the trigger until he could acquire a replacement.

Fixing a Sick Trigger

There are two ways to fix a sick trigger. Work it or replace it. Most competent gunsmiths can improve trigger function. On average they will charge about a hundred bucks for the work. And you shouldn't trust just anyone to do the work. Shooters looking to work their rifle's trigger should resist the urge to tamper with the mechanism themselves unless they are extremely trigger savvy. It should also be mentioned that "work" and "adjust" are two different operations. Most replacement triggers, and a few factory triggers, are shooter adjustable, but what I'm talking about here is modifying the trigger to produce consistent performance.

Trigger Terminology

TRIGGER: The part of a firearm's mechanism designed to be moved by the finger in order to cause the firearm to discharge or fire.

OVERTRAVEL: The distance a trigger moves after the sear has been released.

CREEP: The distance a trigger moves while in contact with the sear.

PULL WEIGHT: The amount of force applied to the trigger to cause sear or hammer release.

SEAR ENGAGEMENT: Measurement of the contact area between the sear and trigger or trigger bar.

TRIGGER BAR: Connecting piece between the trigger and sear. ■

Trigger Consistency

Trigger	Peak Force (Pounds)	Variance (Pounds)	Variance (Percent)	Take-Up (Inches)	Overtravel (Inches)	100-Yard Accuracy (Bench/Offhand) (Inches)
Remington Model 700 ADL						
Factory Remington	6.210	1.159	19	0.006	.092	2.63/9.10
Timney	2.103	.071	3	0.00	.019	1.91/6.22
Timney Prototype*	1.183	.013	1	0.00	.019	2.11/5.91
*The Timney prototype trigger has coated surfaces.						

The good news is that in most cases a dependable aftermarket trigger can be had for about the same price as a trigger job, and if you have the skill to start a fire without gasoline you can do the work yourself. I just recently replaced a trigger in a Remington Model 700 Sendero with a new unit from Timney that comes with the safety already installed. Installation took less time than it does to change the oil in my Dodge Dakota, and the trigger pull weight dropped from an average of 5.4 pounds to a consistent 2.78 pounds. Pull weight variance decreased from almost a pound to less than a tenth of a pound.

Consistency Is the Word

For a trigger to work properly it should break or release the sear crisply. This has been described as

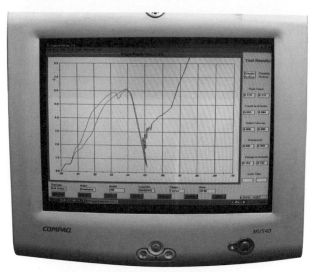

TriggerScan was used to evaluate the consistency of factory and aftermarket triggers. The data was transferred to a home computer where it was displayed as a graph. The graph was also printed out on a computer printer.

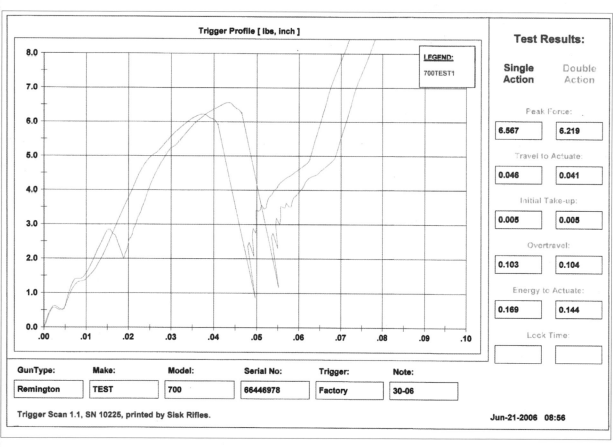

"breaking like a glass rod." This "break" and the trigger movement should be consistent to help your finger learn or develop a memory of how the trigger feels. Consistent is the operative word and is the performance criterion precision-minded shooters strive for in everything from ammunition to optics.

10 Trigger Truths

1. All triggers are not created equal.
2. Engagement surface hardness influences trigger life.
3. Engagement surface slickness influences trigger feel.
4. The color of the trigger does not matter, even if it is gold.
5. Many triggers can be worked/tuned.
6. Triggers on most factory rifles will benefit from being tuned.
7. Most shooters are capable of installing or adjusting aftermarket triggers.
8. Few shooters are capable of correctly modifying a factory trigger.
9. Shooters communicate to their rifles via the trigger.
10. A good trigger helps you shoot better. ■

Handheld Trigger Gauges

Handheld trigger gauges are useful for determining an ostensible pull weight, but in reality they are not adequate for trigger evaluation. With extreme care and perseverance you can see if a trigger is somewhat consistent with a handheld gauge. If you are an experienced shooter, you can do about as well with your finger. As it pertains to good shooting, trigger pull weight is not as important as trigger consistency. That said, handheld gauges can be helpful. If you are using a handheld gauge, make sure you position it on the trigger the same way every time and make sure you apply force evenly and consistently for each test. Don't hold the rifle in one hand and the trigger pull gauge in the other. It's best to have the rifle held in some form of rest like the Tipton Best Gun Vise or similar unit. ■

Some claim precision shooting requires a trigger that exhibits minimal resistance. I have a New Ultra Light Arms Model 20 RF rifle in .22 LR that I use for the majority of my offhand practice. I typically run about 50 rounds a week through it. When shooting my best I can keep five shots inside two inches at 50 yards from a standing, offhand position. The trigger is set at 2.5 pounds, a weight I find comfortable. I have adjusted the trigger to as high as 4 pounds and as low as 1.5 pounds with no appreciable difference in performance. This is because the trigger breaks crisply and consistently at whatever weight it is set.

Shooters should find the pull weight they are comfortable with, and this will depend partly on personal preference and partly on the application of the rifle. A rifle used for prairie dogs or for bench shooting—in other words, one that is often fired from a sturdy rest—will appreciate a light trigger, perhaps 1.5 pounds. A general big-game rifle might prefer a pull weight from 2.5 to 4.5 pounds, and a rifle used in extreme cold with gloved hands or in high-stress, life-and-death situations might be best served with an even heavier pull weight.

Testing Trigger Consistency

To illustrate the importance of consistency in trigger operation I used the Dvorak TriggerScan to conduct a number of trigger tests. TriggerScan is an electronic trigger-pull measuring device that records pull weight, creep, overtravel, and even locktime for rifles and handguns. A rifle cradle or rest is available that will hold the rifle and the measuring unit to eliminate all human influence. The cool part is that TriggerScan automatically transfers the data from each test directly to your computer where it is displayed on a graph, giving you a "trace" of the trigger's operation.

The first trigger test involved a Remington Model 700 ADL in .30-06. I evaluated the factory trigger, an off-the-shelf replacement trigger from Timney, and a prototype Timney trigger with coated surfaces. The results are listed in the chart on page 66. The most striking difference is in the variance or consistency of the triggers. The rifle was also fired for accuracy using factory Winchester 180-grain Power-Point ammunition. Ninety shots were fired from the bench and offhand to test the trigger's influence on accuracy. As the results show, a poor trigger is much easier to manage from a solid rest because the shooter can focus on trigger pull and not divide his attention between that and wobbly sight alignment. Offhand is a different story, and it's where it will become bloody difficult to make a bad trigger behave.

Similar tests with similar results were conducted with other rifles to include 200 rounds fired from the bench from a CZ Model 452 in .17 HMR where a consistent trigger reduced the average group size at 50 yards by 20 percent and greatly reduced the occurrence of flyers. These investigations in conjunction with my experiences with other rifles and the many shooters I have instructed using triggers of various quality show precisely why a good trigger on a rifle is crucial to precision shooting. There are too many other distractions—wind, distance, poor shooting positions, and adrenalin-inducing big antlers—for the shooter to manage a trigger that will provide an unpredictable release.

One of the worst things new shooters can do is train with a terrible trigger. And skilled shooters who have accepted atrocious triggers and maybe lived with one for years should kick those triggers to the curb and find new replacements. I promise that after one date with a good trigger you will be a happier shooter!

PART III
TACTICS FOR LONG-RANGE

ROAD MAP TO
LONG-RANGE

SUCCESS

BY J. GUTHRIE

Want to go long on your next hunt, in a competition, or just for fun?
Here's a road map on how to get it done efficiently.

Back in the day, whenever that was, 300 yards was the outdoor benchmark that got you into "long-range" territory. Much like catching a 10-pound bass or shooting a 10-point buck, sending a bullet precisely on its way the length of three football fields was quite the feat. This day and age, I have rifles that are zeroed at 500 yards, a mere starting point 200 yards beyond the old long-range benchmark.

The shooting world has gone long-range crazy, and rifles, equipment, optics, and ammunition have improved to the point where a novice that can hold a rifle correctly, look through a scope correctly, and squeeze the trigger can hit targets at ranges only a serious competitor or trained marksman would have attempted a few decades ago. I was recently at a seminar where Remington and Leupold had their new Modular Sniper Rifle in .338 Lapua, a fancy variable scope with an even fancier Horus reticle, and a big pile of ammo out for a few writers to shoot. A Leupold employee, who had only just started shooting, was quick to jump into line. She settled in and with the slightest bit of instruction was making head shots on steel targets at 400 yards. If you want to go long, there has never been a better time.

There are all kinds of long-range shots to be made—chasing mule deer out West, in a sniper competition, or even across a hayfield just for fun—but they all require planning if you want to hit the target and not just burn up ammo. I called up friend and shooting mentor Caylen Wojcik to get his thoughts on a basic long-range road map. Of the dozens of friends I have who are long-range shooters, Wojcik offers a truly unique perspective. He spent his formative years as a Marine scout/sniper (arguably some of the best trained long-range shooters in the word), worked as a scout/sniper instructor at the division level, and served as a sniper in combat until a rocket knocked him out of the Battle of Fallujah. Though serious injuries prevented him from returning to combat, the Corps tapped him to train Marines, SEALs, and other Special Forces operators at the 1st Special Operations Training Group sniper school.

After Wojcik turned in his M-40 for the last time and returned home to Washington State, the instructor bug had bitten hard, and he started Central Cascade Precision (CCP). The dozen or so courses he offers each year allow him to pass his expertise on to civilians like myself. We met last summer at one of his courses, and what I learned fundamentally changed my shooting forever—and for the better. Wojcik shoots in sniper competitions and is a serious high-country hunter. His long-range shooting skills have been

A good shooting course will expose you to new and old technologies. Here, a shooter plots targets in a data book after working up the wind call with his iPhone.

applied in combat, hunting, and competition, and he is darn good at teaching others what he knows in an unassuming, precise way.

We divided the long-range game into three basic parts—equipment, training, and mind-set—and sought to pass along some pointers that would help anyone get started, regardless of whether the shots would come at a critter, steel, or scumbag.

Equipment

While it is certainly true that there is more in the man than the rifle, a good rifle—the right good rifle—and other associated equipment are critical to long-range shooting. Wojcik said to go long there is a circle of components, made of four parts, and all are interdependent on one another. Two adjectives should apply to the rifle, ammo, optics, and shooter: consistent and repeatable. If any one part is not consistent and repeatable, hang it up and go home.

"Consistency equals accuracy, and there is no way to cut corners," Wojcik said.

I could fill every page of *Shooting Times* for the next 20 years with a discussion of what rifle in what caliber was the best, settle nothing, and probably start a fight or two. Regardless of barrelmaker and stockmaker, the rifle must be as accurate as your wallet can stand, and it has to be repeatable. And do not forsake what is already in the gun safe.

"I've had students come to my long-range courses with an off-the-shelf .30-06 and shoot really well out to 600 or 700 yards," Wojcik said. "You don't have to drop $4,000 on a rifle. A factory Remington 700 Sendero or Savage are more than capable of providing repeatable results."

But all things being equal, lying down behind an "average" G.A. Precision or Nighthawk custom rifle will allow you to hit smaller targets, much smaller targets, farther away than the average factory rifle. A half-minute of dispersion at 100 yards—a half-inch that will cost you an extra $1,000 or much more—is the difference between a hit or a miss on a 10-inch target at 700 yards.

Caliber is a huge consideration, and a cartridge's performance needs to match your goals, though moving up and down between bullet weights can dramatically increase range. Most of my class members shot .308s for convenience—good ammo is easy to find, and there is a lot of long-range data floating around for .30-caliber bullets—but there was a dramatic difference between those of us shooting 175-grain bullets instead of the lighter and more common 168-grain bullets. It is my guess that we were able to double our hits past 900 yards. If you are stretching a caliber to its absolute limits and not getting the results you want, step up in horsepower. The price is recoil and cost, but if adding another 300 yards to your effective range is a must, it is the only way to go.

No discussion of caliber is complete without discussing loaded ammo. Buy the best you can. My long-range class was the perfect example. Some friends down the line were shooting white box stuff instead of match ammo, and the rounds simply were not consistent or repeatable enough to get hits past 700 yards. The shooter, rifle, and optic were capable of making the shot, but the ammo was not.

"Handloaders can produce match-grade ammo and save a little money

Caylen Wojcik (center), founder of Central Cascade Precision, is a talented long-range shooter and Marine scout/sniper, but most importantly he is an excellent teacher.

in the process," Wojcik said. "It is a fantastic way to extract potential out of your circle of components."

It also allows you more flexibility with a given caliber. Wojcik loads 210-grain Berger VLD hunting bullets and 208-grain Hornady A-Max bullets in his .308 for hunting, weights that are not available in loaded ammunition. The heavier bullet weights extend his range another 200 yards.

Just like ammo and rifle, buy the best optic you can. Figure out what you can afford and then double it, even if it means delaying that range debut for another two or three months. Everyone in our class had good glass, mostly Leupold, Night-Force, and one Schmidt & Bender, and none of us had any problems with repeatability. There are some tremendous scopes on the market—Premier, U.S. Optics, Zeiss, etc.—all of which have different features and prices. It is a matter of doing the research and matching the right scope to your long-range aspirations. You do not need, if only shooting out to 700 or 800 yards, that 34mm

Good optics are a must if you are playing the long-range game—you cannot shoot what you cannot see. Repeatability is another absolute must.

ing reticles on the line instantly obsolete, which brought Wojcik to another important point. Technology, notably laser rangefinders; handheld weather centers; and PDAs, Droids, or iPhones loaded with the latest ballistic software, almost completely eliminate questions of bullet trajectory and can really cut corners on wind calls. If you are inputting accurate bullet velocities (not nominal figures off a theoretical ballistics chart) and accurate atmospheric data, the little computer will tell

id equipment you can depend on," Wojcik said. "I want to buy gear and not worry about it. And don't let something that looks tactical or ninjafied fool you into buying junk. Just because it says it on the box, doesn't mean it is so."

Training

If you are really serious about long-range shooting, go to a good shooting course. It will push your boundaries and your equipment's boundaries, get you out of the comfort zone, and show you the path to dramatic improvement. Humility is a wonderful thing (a tool in itself), and a good shooting course is a heaping spoonful of humility. I am a decent trigger puller; Wojcik made me much better. Wojcik also showed me I am pretty lousy at reading the wind, and that is what really counts out past 500 or 600 yards. I carried an anemometer around for a month afterwards and watched trees, grass, mirage, and dust in an effort to improve my baseline knowledge for wind calls.

The catch is sorting through all the dozens and dozens of available courses. I have met some truly gifted shooters who can hit anything almost anywhere but who could not teach a class of first graders to tie their shoes, much less shoot long range. We all, hopefully, had gifted teachers in school that really

"Just remember that good long-range shooters are repeatable and can always make that shot twice."

tube with all that adjustment range.

Most high-end optics have scads of reticle and turret options, and they all work pretty well after you read through the manual and get some practice. My Nighthawk rifle was equipped with a NightForce 5.5-22X 50mm with my favorite open mil-dot reticle that had served me well out to 600 yards or so. I found during ranging exercises I had a much harder time getting precise ranges with the reduced number of reticle reference points when compared to my fellow shooters who had Horus grids or Leupold TMR reticles.

In practical terms, my laser rangefinder rendered all the rangefind-

you exactly where that bullet will land. We, for all intents and purposes, skipped most of the old-school data gathering during our course, only checking bullet drops against our program-generated drop charts at three points on our way out to 1,000 yards. The program never missed my elevation corrections more than a half-minute. President Reagan's favorite Russian proverb was "trust but verify," so we always double-check the data, but it is usually on the money.

Wojcik had a few other tips on hardware.

"Buy once, cry once—spend the extra $50 to get good gear, rock-sol-

brought a subject to life and made us understand. Long-range shooting instructors need the same kind of skills, not 100 confirmed kills.

"Look at the course curriculum and see if it fits your needs," Wojcik said. "A good student/instructor ratio is 1:15. Also try to go into a school with a clean slate. You don't know what that instructor has up his sleeve that can greatly improve your shooting."

Instructors should be glad to provide you with references and if they will not, that should be an immediate red flag.

Training courses provide a foundation for future training, so be sure to learn the trade before trying the tricks. How much training you do after your training, like everything else in the long-range game, really depends on how serious you are and how you intend to apply what you have learned.

"If you want to maintain proficiency as a competitor or long-range hunter, you need to shoot at least once a month at range under field conditions similar to those that you will face in the field," Wojcik said. "It's tough to put a round count on something like that. I like 150 rounds per day, but that may not be realistic for some people."

Mind-Set

The good news is that any problems that arise on the line or in the field are seldom the fault of a good rifle, scope, or ammunition. The bad news is that any problems that arise on the line or in the field are seldom the fault of a good rifle, scope, or ammunition. Most problems and misses begin and end with the guy squeezing the trigger. Long-range shooting is mostly between the shooter's ears.

"There are guys who show up to my courses, start having a bad day, and immediately blame it on their rifle or scope," Wojcik said. "You have to break it down for them

The ability to shoot little groups off a bench does not translate into the ability to shoot long range in the field. Wojcik stresses shooting in the field and from positions other than prone.

and say, 'Hey man, there is nothing wrong with your equipment.' Know that you are going to miss and accept the fact. Good long-range shooters will identify why they fail and work towards making sure it doesn't happen again. Mind-set relates to training, knowing your capabilities and limitations."

A good long-range shooter also knows when to quit. The superbly accurate Nighthawk Custom rifle I used during Wojcik's course is more than capable of hitting the vitals of an elk at 1,000 yards, provided I make the right wind call. Would I ever shoot an elk that far just because? Absolutely not.

"My .308 runs out of killing gas at around 600 yards," Wojcik said. "Could I shoot animals at a farther distance? Yes, but why risk it? Take ethical, responsible shots. Know your lethal distance. Buying up in caliber and equipment doesn't buy you distance."

If paper or steel are on the receiving end of a bullet strike and you can afford the ammo, go for it. Just remember that good long-range shooters are repeatable and can always make that shot twice.

I recently filmed an episode for Modern Rifle Adventures in Colorado. We were hunting antelope, and I was using a DPMS competition rifle in 6.5mm Creedmoor, one of my favorite new calibers. The rifle,

though not ideal for lugging across the high plains, was very accurate and averaged 3.5-inch groups at 300 yards. I knew my dope to the quarter-minute out to 400 and also knew that sitting, off shooting sticks, I could still hold 6-inch groups. When my heavy-horned buck walked up out of a coulee at 314 yards, there was a slight wind and no hesitation. Good equipment defined a "mechanical" margin of error. Training allowed me to maximize the system's inherent accuracy and, more importantly, defined my limitations. Mind-set gave me the confidence to make the shot.

Learn, Shoot, Smile

Wojcik is one of the best firearms instructors I've ever met, period. If you want to learn the basics or more advanced long-range techniques, the courses he teaches at Central Cascade Precision (ccptraining.com) are a great place to start. In addition to basic long-range marksmanship, he also offers a high-angle course, a designated marksman course for AR shooters, and a hunter's course. I'm not in the business of issuing unqualified endorsements, but CCP and Wojcik get an unqualified endorsement from me. Go, learn, hit little targets at obscene distances, and smile all the way home.

Stop Guessing the Wind

By Zak Smith

Lightweight, affordable, reliable wind meters are helping to take some of the guesswork out of mid- to long-range shooting.

Much of tactical shooting is focused on engaging targets at close range, with pistol, rifle and shotgun. At these short distances, the shooter can ignore the atmosphere; the wind isn't going to blow his 9mm bullet off target before it impacts the 10-yard target, nor will it deflect his 5.56mm bullet before it impacts a 50-yard target. In these scenarios

wind, temperature, and altitude or pressure changes will not affect his ability to deliver hits on target.

For the precision long-range shooter employing a bolt-action sniper rifle, however, monitoring the wind and environment is critical to making hits. Both law enforcement and military employment of precision rifles is such that first-round hits are paramount; shooting mul-

tiple rounds is often unacceptable because the target will be alerted to the shooter's presence and react.

The environment changes the bullet's path in basically two ways. The first is wind. Wind is ever-present, with totally calm conditions being rare. Wind primarily affects the bullet's path by pushing it left or right. Winds pushing the bullet up or down are rare, unless there are intervening terrain features such that a strong crosswind is deflected up. A light wind of five mph going straight left to right will deflect the path of a .308 by about three inches at 300 yards.

The second way the environment affects the path is by slowing the bullet's velocity due to air friction or drag. The drag on a bullet is higher the faster it goes, which means that a bullet starts out at a high velocity from the muzzle but rapidly slows. As the bullet slows, the rate of deceleration slows as well. If the atmosphere has a higher density, which means the air is thicker, the bullet will slow more rapidly than in thin air. This means that a bullet will decelerate faster on a cold day at sea level than it will on a hot day at 7,000 feet altitude in the mountains. As soon as the bullet leaves the muzzle, gravity tugs it downward, which makes it drop more the farther it travels. Since a bullet in a thicker atmosphere will take longer to get to 500 yards than the same bullet fired in a thin atmosphere, the one fired in the thin atmosphere will have less drop than the one in the thick atmosphere. The ultimate effect of atmospheric density for the shooter is that his drop tables will change based on the density of the air.

In summary, if station pressure goes down, altitude goes up, temperature goes up or humidity goes up, then the air gets less dense and provides less resistance to the bullet. On the other hand, if pressure goes up, altitude goes down, temperature goes down or humidity goes down, the air gets more dense and provides more resistance to the bullet.

What does all this mean in practical terms? The precision long-range rifle shooter needs to accurately estimate wind and keep track of environmental conditions in order to make first-round hits. Thankfully, there are some technological tools available that ease this task. The most basic tool is the handheld wind meter (or anemometer), which can measure the wind speed at the shooter's position.

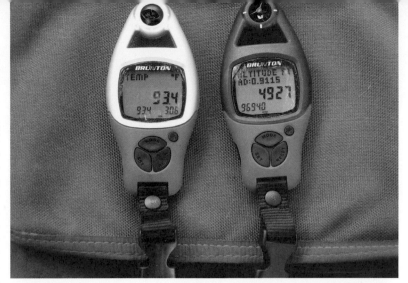

The Brunton units display a lot of information and are handy, but they lack impeller protection.

Handheld environmental stations can provide the long-range shooter with information key to making the shot.

The benefit of the wind meter is that it provides the shooter with an accurate measure of wind velocity; however, the big limitation is that it only provides information about the current position. Wind is often different from one location to the next, and the bullet may pass through several different wind conditions along its path. If the wind at the shooter is three mph left to right but it switches to 10 mph right to left 100 yards downrange, a left hold calculated at the shooter's position will result in a miss.

Even with this limitation, the handheld wind meter can provide a baseline wind condition on which the shooter can base his downrange corrections. Also, after playing around getting wind readings in different conditions, the shooter will eventually learn what wind indicators such as tactile feel, grass and leaf deflection,

Making hits at long range requires accurate range estimation, ballistic data, and environmental monitoring.

and mirage correspond to in terms of wind speed in mph. By correlating what five mph "feels like," he is better prepared to accurately guess wind conditions in the future.

As the shooter arrives at his position, he pulls gear out of his drag bag such as his data book, rangefinder, shooting support, and in some cases additional concealment material. As he builds his range card, it is a good time to whip out the wind meter to take a baseline reading of direction and wind speed and annotate it on the card. As he waits and observes,

he needs to keep track of local wind changes and make judgements about wind conditions downrange.

But wind is just one part of the total environment. For long-range shooting, keeping track of the altitude, temperature, and station pressure—the parameters that affect long-range trajectory the most—can mean the difference between a hit and a miss. For shooters who travel often, changes in altitude are critical. At zero feet above sea level, a typical .308 load drops 213 inches at 800 yards, but at 5,000 feet altitude, it

only drops 194 inches—a difference of almost 2 1/2 minutes of angle.

Stepping up from the basic wind meter, there are several portable environmental stations available to the long-range shooter. Some, such as the Speedtech Skymaster, offer temperature or altitude, while top-end models like the Kestrel 4000 measure and report just about every atmospheric parameter one could wish for. I got my hands on nine different devices for evaluation.

La Crosse instruments has a very simple and inexpensive Handheld

WIND METER FEATURES BY MODEL

Manufacturer	Model	Wind	Temp	RH	Station Pressure	Altitude	Density Altitude	Impeller Protector	Ease of use	Price
La Crosse	Handheld Anemometer	X	X						**	$55
Extech	Mini-Anemometer	X	X	X				X	*	$129
Speedtech	Skymaster SM-28	X	X	X	X	X		X	*	$190
Brunton	ADC Wind	X	X						**	$80
Brunton	ADC Pro	X	X	X	X	X	X		**	$200
Kestrel	1000	X						X	***	$74
Kestrel	2500	X	X		X	X		X	***	$149
Kestrel	3000	X	X	X				X	***	$149
Kestrel	4000	X	X	X	X	X	X	X	***	N/A

Note: Some atmospheric measurements that are not relevant to long-range trajectory were omitted from this table, such as heat index and wind chill.

SOURCES

Brunton
(800) 443-4871
www.brunton.com

Extech Instruments
(877) 239-8324
www.extech.com

La Crosse Instruments
(608) 785-7939
www.lacrossetechnology.com

Nielsen-Kellerman (Kestrel)
(610) 447-1555
www.nkhome.com

Speedtech Instruments
(866) 670-5982
www.weatherhawk.com

At the Pawnee National Grasslands, where it is easy to find 1,000-yard distances and strong winds, this shooter tries to get a handle on the current conditions.

Anemometer for about $55. It is the most compact of the units tested and the cheapest. It can be used to effectively monitor both the wind speed and the temperature and is pretty easy to operate.

Extech's Mini Thermo-Anemometer measures wind speed, temperature, and relative humidity. Its physical size is among the largest of the reviewed units.

Speedtech's Skymaster looks and operates very like the Extech, but it can also measure station pressure and altitude. Both of these units have fold-out protective cases, which cover the impeller, sensors, and controls. Their downside is that the controls are less user-friendly than some of the other units tested.

Brunton was next in line with its ADC Wind and ADC Pro. The Wind model displays wind speed and temperature. The Pro model measures everything of interest: wind speed, temperature, relative humidity, pressure, altitude, and density altitude. The Brunton units are easy to use and compact in size. Unfortunately, their impeller is not protected by an external cover and might be more prone to damage than some of the other wind meters. The LCD display scrolls through the different measurements, but most screens have three or four parameters displayed. This method of display can be a little confusing if you are looking for one number in a hurry.

Kestrel offers the widest array of handheld wind meters and portable environmental stations appropriate for field shooting. Starting out, the Kestrel model 1000 measures only wind speed. The next model up that I tested was the 2500, which displays wind speed, temperature, station pressure, and altitude. The model 3000 additionally displays relative humidity but not station pressure or altitude. Finally, the model 4000 [now the model 5000] is the most full-featured environmental station for shooting that I tested. It measures not just wind speed, temperature, relative humidity, pressure, and altitude but density altitude as well. The 1000 to 3000 models all have a slip-off plastic cover to protect the face of the device, while the 4000 has a flip-off impeller cover; the controls and LCD are not protected. The Kestrel units had the most straightforward operation and easiest-to-read displays of all the tested devices. The 4000 is available with a night-vision-compatible backlight in the 4000 NV.

Which Is Right for You?

If you want full wind, temperature, altitude and density altitude, there are only two choices: the Brunton ADC Pro and the Kestrel 4000. Of those, I prefer the 4000 because it is easier to read and has more features. If its price is too steep, the ADC Pro does the job. If all you need is a wind and temperature measurement device, the La Crosse Handheld Anemometer cannot be beat for the price.

INVIS

INFLUENCE

A wind formula you can actually use in the field.
BY JEFF HOFFMAN

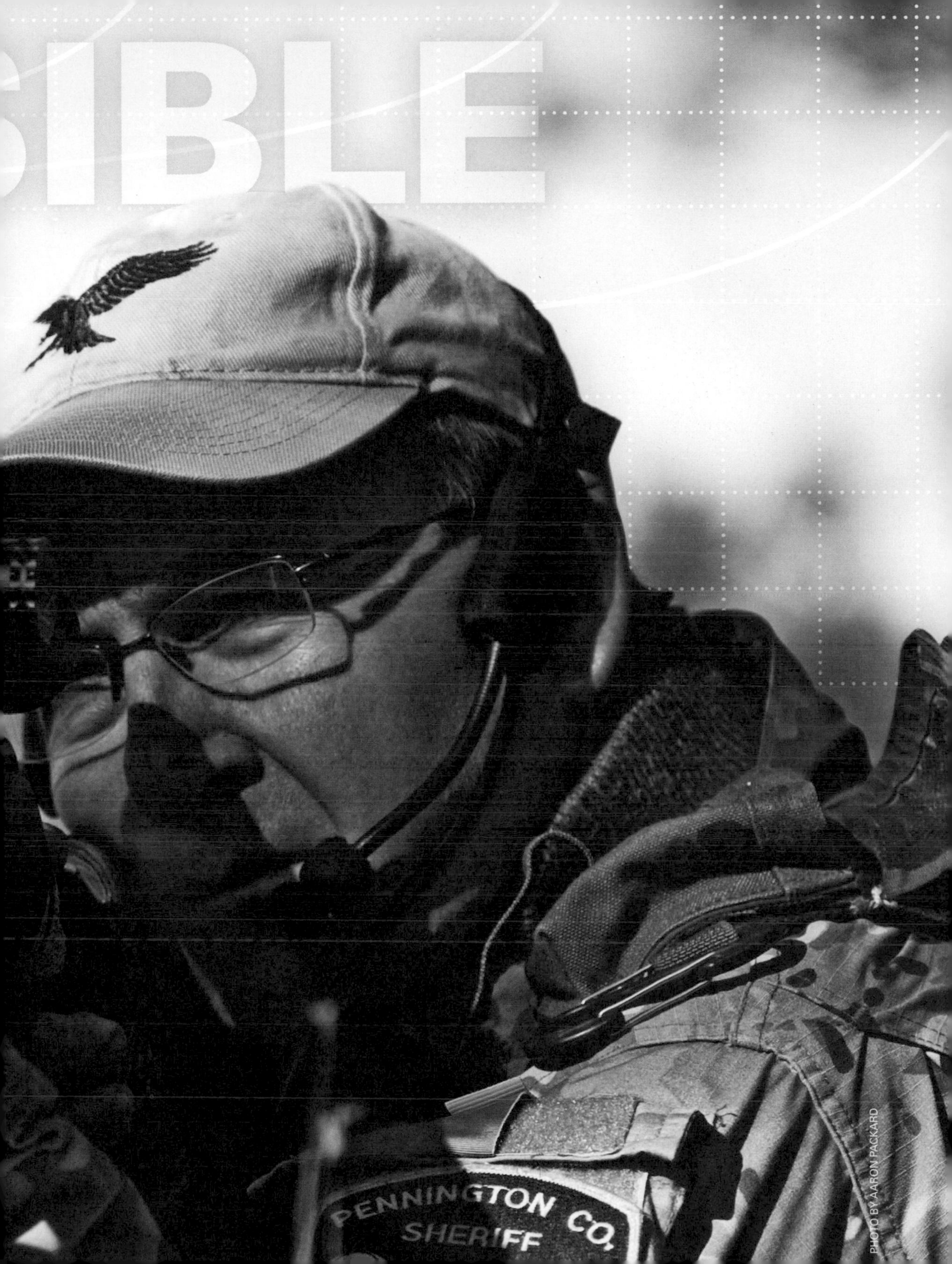
SIBLE
PENNINGTON CO.
SHERIFF
PHOTO BY AARON PACKARD

A critical component of shooting accurately in the wind is accurately measuring wind speed. A Kestrel handheld weather station accomplishes this task magnificently.

PHOTO BY DoD

A sniper needs to accurately measure, then compensate for, wind. He needs a formula to calculate wind effect that is easily remembered and can be utilized quickly in the field without looking at charts or using a calculator.

Someone once said, "The amateur is concerned with trajectory. The professional is concerned with wind effect." He's right. Trajectory is relatively predictable because gravity doesn't change. Wind effect changes not only with range, but also with the velocity of the wind and the angle relative to the path of the bullet.

To be effective at long range, a sniper needs to be able to accurately predict and compensate for the effect of prevailing wind upon his bullet. To do this he needs a formula for accurately calculating the wind effect that is easily remembered and can be utilized quickly in the field without looking at charts or using a calculator. There is a standard U.S. military formula that all serious snipers have seen. I won't go into details over it except to say that I can't use it in the field, and I have heard the same from snipers on the

most skilled and respected teams in the world. It is simply too difficult to complete without a calculator.

A few years ago a fellow law enforcement sniper and I entered a competition held for both police and military snipers. As police snipers, we did well out to 400 yards, but at longer distances we had our butts handed to us by military snipers who had more experience shooting in wind. Humility is a great motivator, so when I got back, I had steel targets made and started shooting long range in the wind. I also sat in front of a computer screen with a ballistics program and studied the trajectory and effect of wind on a .308 match projectile at various ranges.

My goal was to find a simplified formula that could be used in the field, quickly and while under stress. The formula I came up with is relatively quick, uses very basic math, and is easily remembered and used in the field without resorting to charts, notes, and calculators.

Three Basic Steps

This formula provides the firing solution in terms of minutes of angle (MOA) and is for the .308

Match and 7.62x51 NATO sniping rounds, such as M118LR. It allows you to either dial in the correction or hold off using mil-dot spaces as reference.

It has three basic steps:

1. Make your initial calculation based on a 10-mph full-value wind.

2. Adjust for actual wind speed.

3. Adjust for actual wind value.

You can't accurately compensate for wind effect unless you can accurately estimate wind speed. For this, you need an accurate wind gauge. I highly recommend the basic Kestrel-brand unit, the Kestrel 1000. You should practice with it to the point that you can reliably feel and observe wind in field conditions and know what the actual wind velocity is based on your observations. With practice, you will be able to call wind speed accurately without use of the wind gauge. This is important because our goal is to be fast and accurate, without any crutches. Your target won't

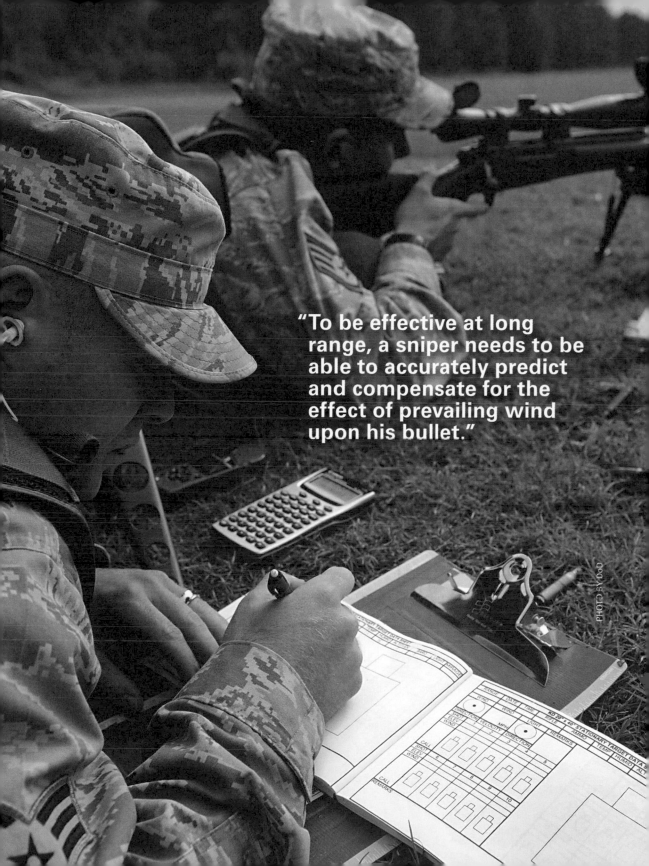

"To be effective at long range, a sniper needs to be able to accurately predict and compensate for the effect of prevailing wind upon his bullet."

wait while you are digging for stuff to help with your calculations.

The Formula

The formula I came up with is:

Range (in yards, expressed as a single digit) – 1 = x MOA of correction needed (based on a 10-mph full-value wind).

Example: If you intend to hit a target 700 yards away, you would need to allow 6 minutes of wind correction: 7-1= 6. If you had an 800-yard target, you would need 7 minutes of correction: 8-1=7. If you had a 500-yard target, you would need 4 minutes of correction: 5-1=4.

That's the first step, again, regardless of actual existing wind speed or value. Next, you need to adjust for actual wind speed and actual wind value. It makes no difference in which order you do the next two steps.

Actual Wind Speed

Wind will deflect the bullet in direct proportion to the speed of the wind. A 20-mph wind affects the bullet exactly twice as much as a 10-mph wind. A 5-mph wind will deflect the bullet one-half as much as a 10-mph wind. A 15-mph wind will deflect the bullet 50 percent more than a 10-mph wind. This makes it easy for us to use the basic formula and alter it to be accurate under conditions

PHOTO BY DoD

where the wind is something other than 10 mph.

Example: You are shooting at a target 700 yards away with a 5-mph, full-value wind. Do the basic formula: 7-1=6 MOA of correction. Because you are shooting in a 5-mph wind, not a 10-mph wind, adjust your calculation by cutting the estimated wind deflection by one half: 6÷2=3 MOA of correction needed.

I put wind into increments of 3, 5, 7, 10, 15, and 20. I like 3 as correction because I have a tough time remembering all the wind-speed indicators, such as leaves blowing and trees swaying, but I know that if I can feel a wind on my face, it is worth at least a 3-mph compensation.

One way of compensating for winds that are a fraction of the basic 10-mph wind is to take your initial calculation made for a 10-mph wind and multiply it by .3, .7, etc. If our target is 700 yards away, with a 3-mph wind, the calculation might look like this: 7-1=6, 6x.3=1.8 MOA of correction needed. Scopes don't allow for an exact 1.8 MOA correction, so we dial in 1.75 MOA, 2 MOA, or hold off one-half mil. All will result in a hit.

Actual Wind Value

The formula we are using here is based (for the initial calculation) on a full-value wind. Not all winds

are full value. For the last step we need to adjust for the actual wind value. Many sniper schools teach only three wind values: full value (a wind perpendicular to the path of the bullet), no value (running the same angle as the path of the bullet, either straight to you or straight away from you), and half value. They teach that everything between full and no value is half value. This is too rough for my taste. It may put you on a human-size target out to 600 yards, but to hit past that or to hit with more precision, you should break it down more precisely. More important, a primary assumption of this teaching is wrong. A perfect 45-degree wind has a three-quarter value, not a half value, as most schools teach. (A 45-degree wind actually has a true effect of .707, so you can do the math by using three-quarters of your calculation to this point, or you can make the math a little easier and multiply by .7, which is what I do.) A 30-degree wind is a true half value.

So how do we use actual wind value? You need to take the result of your calculation up to this point and adjust it for actual wind value. Let's put it all together.

Example: Assume you have a target at 700 yards with a 5-mph wind intersecting the line from you to the target at a 45-degree angle. What is the correction needed?

15° = 1/4 VALUE

30° = 1/2 VALUE

45° = 3/4 VALUE

65° = 9/10 VALUE

90° = FULL VALUE

NO VALUE

Fine-tuning wind values

Step 1: Since the target is at 700, we know we need 6 MOA of correction for Step 1 (7-1=6).

Step 2: It's a 5-mph wind, so we cut that number in half to get 3 MOA (6÷2=3).

Step 3: Because the wind is at 45 degrees, we need to multiply the 3 MOA by .7 to get 2.1.

We use .7 because a 45-degree wind affects the bullet only 70 percent of what it would if it were a perfect full-value wind: 3x.7=2.1. Obviously, we round this to 2 MOA of correction needed.

Tips

This formula is caliber-specific for .308 175-grain Match or 7.62 M118LR. It works well for .308 168-grain Match, but the 168-grain Match is an inferior choice for distances past 600 yards.

Not all targets you are presented with are at even 100-yard increments. I round down to a great extent because the formula tends to err slightly toward overstating wind effect. If the target were at 735 yards, for wind-calculation purposes, I would call it 700, and my first calculation would result in 6 MOA of needed wind correction.

The formula is based on normal atmospheric conditions: sea level to 4,000 feet elevation and, say, zero to 90 degrees F. If you are higher in elevation than that or hotter than that in temperature, the air will be thinner, resulting in less wind deflection. The solution is to change the initial calculation to R-2=x MOA of correction, rather than R-1=x MOA of correction, and proceed from there in the same manner as previously described.

Wind at the shooter's location may not be the same as that at the target or at any point in between. I normally estimate it at my shooting position, then look along the path to the target for indications of wind. What are the grass, trees, and dust doing? What is the mirage doing? What is the terrain along the path? Does the terrain block the wind at some points, or is it likely that the wind is being funneled through at a higher velocity than what I am feeling?

It is important when determining wind angle to try to be precise in your estimate. I don't simply face the target when determining wind angle. I draw an imaginary line between the target and me. I then try to determine the angle at which the wind intersects that line.

Practice with the Formula

Any formula is useless unless you can apply it. You have to practice using it in order to be fast enough to do the math in your head, while under pressure, before the conditions change. You also have to develop the confidence in knowing that it works for you by actually using it in the field.

Spend the money and buy a good wind gauge. If you don't, you're wasting your time because you can't apply the formula unless you know the wind speed. Being able to estimate wind speed comes from practice in the field with the wind gauge.

Remember, wind problems are tough to solve perfectly. If you somehow were able to solve it perfectly, by the time you calculated your answer, the problem would be different because your target would have moved or the wind would have changed in strength or angle. Speed of calculation with a reasonably accurate method is far superior to a perfect answer that arrives too late. You have to be willing to accept some estimation error and some rounding in the interest of speed.

OTHER CALIBERS

Okay, it's a good method, but what if you shoot some other caliber? If you are shooting 5.56 with 77-grain bullets, I have a variation for you. You need to modify Step 1. Instead of Range minus One, simply use R=MOA. This means that whatever range you are shooting at, that is the MOA correction required in a 10-mph wind. At 400 yards you need 4 MOA of correction; at 600 yards you need 6 MOA. This is because the wind affects the 5.56 bullet more, so more correction is needed. This works accurately for 5.56 77-grain ammo out to 600 yards. At that point the bullet has slowed enough that the formula does not give sufficient correction.

This formula can also be used for other calibers by applying a correction factor. The .300 Win. Mag. with a 190-grain Match bullet is affected only 70 percent as much as a .308 175-grain bullet. You can do the calculations as Step 4: multiply by .7 to adjust for the lesser wind drift of the .300 Win. Mag. projectile. Similarly, the .338 Lapua has a .6 correction factor, and the .50 BMG has a .4 correction factor.

—Jeff Hoffman

Dial or Hold?

A lot of shooters debate the merits of dialing in corrections with turrets or holding off with a reticle.

Which system is best?

BY J. GUTHRIE

As hunters and shooters look to increase their range, accuracy, and speed, lots of questions come to the fore. Which rifle is the most accurate? Which caliber is the flattest shooting and hits the hardest? Should I reload or shoot factory ammo? As an optics editor, the most frequent question I have been asked of late is, "Should I get a scope with a BDC reticle, mildot reticle, or target turrets—or both?"

A ballistic reticle provides excellent ability to engage multiple targets at various ranges quickly without coming out of the scope. With a lot of practice, the reticle can be used as a ranging device.

It is a straightforward question, but there is no simple answer. Like most answers for firearms questions—from concealed carry to hunting mule deer to making a 1,000-yard shot—it all starts with a big "that depends." And just like the right concealed-carry handgun is vastly different than the rifle needed for hunting, the right optic for a fellow looking to make a fast 400-yard shot on a whitetail is vastly different than the appropriate scope for shooting steel past a mile. Or sometimes it is the same, depending.

In addition to my own experiences, I corralled long-range instructor Todd Hodnett for a couple of hours and got his take on the conundrum. Hodnett trains all levels of the military up through SOCOM for 11 months of the year and sees 10,000 to 15,000 rounds fired at ranges exceeding a mile—and then some—each week. He developed the Horus H58, H59, and TReMoR2 reticles, and he consults for a number of scope companies. All this experience points to one, simple goal—to get rounds on target. Hodnett agreed with some of my assertions, but more importantly, he pointed out some important factors that I had overlooked.

Reasons for Reticles

You can divide reticles into several classes: simple, ballistic drop compensating (BDC), and graduated. Examples for each include a dot or duplex for simple reticles; ballistic drop compensating reticles like the Nikon BDC, Bushnell DOA, and the Zeiss Rapid-Z; and in the graduated category are the mil- or minute-of-angle-based reticles like Leupold's TMR, Trijicon's MOA, and the various Horus grid/dropdown reticles. They all have various applications and limitations.

A reticle's most obvious virtue is simplicity. If properly calibrated and etched into glass, there is nothing to move or break. There are no clicks to count and forget. And reticles are exponentially faster than turrets when it comes to making that first shot or following up with a correction—if you have the right reticle.

For a hunter shooting big game inside of 300 yards on one ranch or farm, there really is no reason for using anything beyond a simple reticle. Even with milder big-game cartridges, a 200-yard zero will allow a fellow to hold on even a smallish whitetail and still drop a bullet through the vitals.

Before the new millennium rolled around, BDC reticles were found mostly on military scopes or were a custom retrofit for serious civilian shooters. Over the years various companies have developed their own BDC reticles and put them in scopes, the Zeiss Rapid-Z, Leupold's Boone & Crockett, Swarovski's TDS, and Nikon's BDC to name a few. The multitude of designs met with varying success, and a lot of that success was dependent on price point. The BDC line of Nikon scopes, for example, covering everything from varmint hunting, plinking with ARs, and muzzleloaders, were, and are, wildly popular mostly because they work.

Nikon relies on some constants to make the circle system accurate at moderate ranges. For example, most muzzleloader hunters use 150 grains of pelletized propellant and shoot a 250-grain bullet nestled in a sabot. And a majority of AR owners shoot 55-grain bullets through carbine-length barrels. But if you read the instructions, Nikon, to its credit, is quick to say it cannot account for all the variables and that its system absolutely must be "ground checked" on the range before hunting.

Therein lies the problem with a BDC reticle. It cannot adapt to changing conditions or a new set of ballistic parameters.

"For the average hunter who understands the capabilities and limitations of a BDC reticle, it is a good option," Hodnett said. "If you extend the range out 600 or 800 yards, then it becomes a problem. That reticle is made for one ballistic coefficient, velocity, and air density. If any of that changes significantly, the reticle isn't worth a hill of beans."

I took one of the newer BDC reticles, paired with a very accurate .338 Lapua rifle, to a prairie dog shoot in Wyoming last summer. The reticle was designed to match the trajectory of 250-grain Hornady A-Max bullets launched at 2,875 fps. My guess is they plugged in 1,000 or 2,000 feet of elevation. On my home range at 10 feet above sea level and out to 300 yards, it was spot on. In Wyoming at 6,000 feet, it was point and shoot out to 400 or so yards. When we set a target board at 1,000 yards, my shots were almost 2 feet over the target. The change in elevation, or air density more specifically, made the reticle practically useless at ranges past 700 yards.

"Here in my home town of Canadian, Texas, we've had temperatures of 118 and -18 degrees in one year," Hodnett said. "For a .308 that amounts to two mils, or 64 inches, of elevation difference at 800 meters. At 300 yards it is no big deal, but when you really need a BDC reticle, that is when they start lying to you."

Another knock against BDC reticles is they only work at one power setting unless they are located in the first focal plane, which until recently, few were.

My biggest problem with simple or BDC reticles is pure accuracy—the ability to subtend or hold a point of aim accurately and consistently. Simple reticles have one point of aim. Most BDC reticles subtend in 50-yard increments, and how often

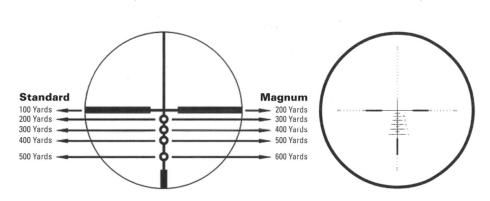

Standard		Magnum
100 Yards		200 Yards
200 Yards		300 Yards
300 Yards		400 Yards
400 Yards		500 Yards
500 Yards		600 Yards

Ballistic drop compensating reticles, such as the Nikon BDC (left) and Zeiss Rapid-Z (right), offer hunters and shooters a way to quickly make shots at distant targets, but they are limited when loads or environmental factors change drastically.

do deer walk out at exactly 450 yards? They pop out at 378 yards or 421 yards, and where exactly is that on a simple or BDC reticle? A .308 rifle firing a 168-grain bullet (2,680 fps, .462 BC, 100-yard zero @ sea level) is 10.3 MOA, or 48.5 inches, low at 450 yards. At 500 yards the same combination is 12.4 MOA, or 64.8 inches, low—a difference of more than 16 inches, half the height of a large whitetail or mule deer.

Sometimes the degree of attainable accuracy is certainly adequate. I have a Nikon Coyote Special 3-9X 40mm on a predator rifle, and with 55-grain ammunition of almost any kind, the circles are close enough for government work out to 300 yards.

I grabbed a very accurate Sabre Defense AR-15, two Leupold scopes, and some ammo to test out the practical accuracy of the two sighting systems. At 300 yards with Black Hills Mk 262 Mod 1 ammo, the rifle's five-shot group average was just over 3 inches. Using the turrets of the first scope (a Leupold Mark 4 4.5-15X 50mm), I could dial in a 4.5 MOA correction and get the rounds in or nearly touching a 2.5-inch dot with every shot. After replacing the Mark 4 with a VX-6 2-12X 42mm with the standard duplex, the feat was much more difficult. Why? I had to guess the elevation correction. Not only was I less likely to hit the dot, my average three-shot group was around 6 inches. It was just impossible to consistently find that magic 4.5 MOA/14.4-inch spot on the vertical stadia.

Hodnett summed it up succinctly, "It is like trying to use a ruler with most of the lines erased."

All this theory gets blown to hell when you use a drop-down reticle like Hodnett's Horus H58 or H59. They look busy to guys who use a duplex, but they are busy for a reason. The grid allows shooters to subtend .2 mil, the same degree of precision offered by most turrets—

and do so almost instantaneously. And make near instant corrections for a follow-up shot. The new TReMoR2 reticle allows shooters to estimate range and hold for elevation and wind in a few seconds. As Hodnett said, "Mil-dots are so 1970s."

If Turrets Were Timely

My first range session with a repeatable set of target turrets was a seminal moment, opening doors that regular scopes had kept locked shut. I could make a bullet go anywhere I wanted in 1/4-MOA increments and come back home with the flick of a wrist. If you buy a good scope, turrets are repeatable and very easy to use. But they do have a few drawbacks.

The biggest are forgetting what you have dialed or accidentally moving the turret. This fall I was "mentoring" a first-time deer hunter. We spotted some does on a field edge 342 yards away, but they slipped past before—you guessed it—I could dial a correction and get settled in for a shot. With plans for a superb display of my field marksmanship later in the morning, I simply left the 6.5 MOA correction on the scope. So when a doe popped out at 75 yards an hour later, I scorched

hair off her back instead of dropping her where she stood. The kid was pretty unimpressed.

I have also dialed in an unwanted windage correction by jogging with my rifle tucked under my arm from one point to another. Another time I lost track of my rotations and managed to miss a prairie dog at 100 yards by, oh, 10 feet. This was an issue for military and police snipers, so the latest generation of sniper scopes have lockable turrets, zero stop, and tactile rotation indicators. These refinements are generally found on only the most expensive units though.

Hodnett stressed that it was critical to make sure that 1/10 mil is actually 1/10 mil and that the mechanical system that moves the reticle around is sound and repeatable. Drills like "shooting the square" and calibration devices like the Horus CATS targets are easy ways to check your scope. And you should check your scopes every year. Both Hodnett and I have seen $3,000 scopes that would not track and $300 units that worked just fine.

Turrets are flexible, and if you keep a data book on your rifle, switching loads is painless. I have a Remington Model 700 Police topped with a turret-equipped

Turrets are repeatable and easy to use, but they have drawbacks. Can you spot the difference here? If not, you missed by 15 inches at 100 yards! The turret is a full revolution off zero with just a little line to tell you so.

Leupold Mark 4 and data that allows me to swap seamlessly between five different loads.

And while reticles are faster, a practiced rifleman running familiar turrets is not exactly slow. Most long-range shooting allows for plenty of setup time. Unlike military snipers who need to make shots fast to avoid getting shot, hunters should absolutely take plenty of time to make sure a rifle is rock steady and double-check range and wind before taking a long-range shot on a game animal. In fact, checking a data book or drop chart and dialing in a correction is the least of my worries when shooting at a game animal at longer ranges.

The thing I love about turrets is the precision with which corrections can be made. I often use an iPod and a ballistic program in conjunction with a Kestrel 3500 NV weather meter to develop firing solutions and elevation and windage corrections. A 1/4-MOA or .2-mil turret allows me to dial exactly what the programs spit out or what the bullets tell me after they strike steel in controlled and repeated fashions.

The Answer

Even after several pages of point and counterpoint, thousands of rounds and hundreds of hours on the shooting line, the answer is still, "It depends."

I am a firm believer that a man cannot have too much capability built into his rifle. That said, it makes little sense for a fellow who hunts whitetails and never takes a shot over 200 yards to have a BDC or drop-down reticle or target turrets. A fixed 4X is probably the solution to all his optical problems.

Though Hodnett and I are not enamored with BDC reticles, they have their place and work just fine, depending. As one of my buddies was quick to say when discussing this report, "If it's 118 or -18 degrees,

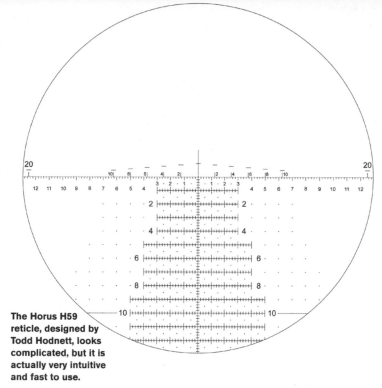

The Horus H59 reticle, designed by Todd Hodnett, looks complicated, but it is actually very intuitive and fast to use.

I'm not going to be out shooting. I'm going to be inside by a fire or sitting under the AC." The guy in the middle, the average shooter shooting an average load in an average rifle, can get by just fine with a BDC reticle—if the ranges are moderate and the conditions are consistent.

My vote is for a scope with an MOA- or mil-based reticle and turrets graduated in the same unit of measure, which can be difficult to get if the search is limited to U.S. manufacturers. (Many scopes have mil-based reticles and MOA adjustments, and it has taken a long time to get manufacturers sorted out.) Having both allows a great deal of flexibility. Depending on the reticle, you could use the turrets to account for different loads and hold off. Or use the turrets for shots when there is time to get settled and the reticle for rushed shots at fleeting targets. Or use both at the same time, getting close with the turrets and then fine-tuning follow-up shots with the reticle. It all depends on the situation.

"I will certainly dial with a first-focal plane scope," Hodnett said. "I might dial five and hold three depending on the circumstances."

Getting on target—steel or flesh and bone—at long ranges takes work and the right equipment.

"A man's capabilities are limited by the effort he puts into it," Hodnett said. "Get out of your comfort zone. The info and equipment are easy to obtain. I've got guys who have never seen my TReMoR2 reticle that end up shooting out past a mile before the course is over. And it happens every week, every training cycle."

The guy who mounts a scope, reads the directions once, and heads to the field is setting himself up to fail. Any system, whether it be a BDC or drop-down reticle or turrets, must be proven through practice. Only then will a rifleman make full advantage of a system's potential.

Accurate Shooting with

from 100 to 1000 Y

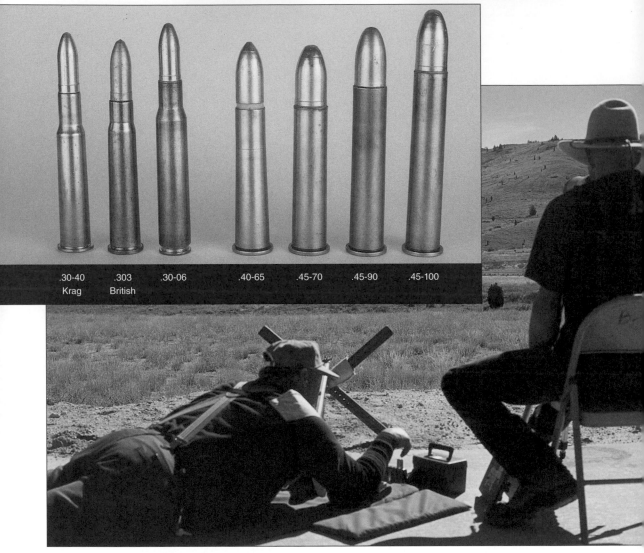

.30-40 Krag   .303 British   .30-06   .40-65   .45-70   .45-90   .45-100

Mike's tips can help you create the most accurate cast-bullet handloads.

BY MIKE VENTURINO
PHOTOS BY YVONNE VENTURINO

B ack in my college years I was poorer than the proverbial church mouse, so there was no big time partying or traipsing off to Florida during spring breaks for this young shooter and handloader. What I did with the small amounts of money I could scrape up was buy some quality guns and the powder and primers needed to shoot them. As for bullets, I made all those myself.

CAST BULLETS

Lone Star Rolling Block

For my rifle shooting I managed to find a Springfield Model 1903A3 .30-06 still in full battle dress. And for a few dollars I acquired a Lyman No. 311291 mold with which to cast 170-grain roundnose gas-checked bullets. I fired thousands of rounds through that rifle, and not even one of them was a factory load or jacketed bullet. It didn't take me long to realize that with the peep sights it was equipped with, I could get my home-cast bullets grouping within a couple of inches at 100 yards. Great fun was had in experimenting with alloy hardness and different powder and primer types.

With that background it's no wonder that even though I can now afford to buy bullets today I still have an extensive bullet mold collection. I can cast bullets for rifles as small as .22 caliber and as large as .58 caliber. It doesn't seem to surprise anyone to hear of good cast bullet accuracy being delivered by big-bore rifles, but I've experienced some fine grouping with cast bullets even from .22 centerfire rifles, such as the .222 Remington and the .220 Swift.

Right now I am loading cast bullets for a wide variety of rifles and shooting them at targets as close as 100 yards and as distant as 1000 yards. The cartridges those rifles are chambered for range from modern bottleneck, smokeless powder rounds to large-bore, straight-sided blackpowder rounds. To achieve success in reloading all these different cartridges with lead-alloy bullets I poured myself requires vastly different techniques and components. But the actual effort expended to prepare good cast-bullet rifle ammunition is just a bit more than when loading good jacketed bullet ammo. And the satisfaction gained from doing all this yourself is immeasurable.

My most recent shooting interest has been in bolt-action military rifles, so in my rifle racks sit U.S. Krags, Model 1903 Springfields, Model 1917 Enfields, and a modest assortment of foreign-made types. The amount of jacketed bullets fired

Cast rifle bullets are not just used for competing in BPCR matches. The author fires them in his old M1903 battle rifles as well.

Lyman No. 311299 .30 Cal. 190-Gr. Semipointed	Lyman No. 314299 .30 Cal. 195-Gr. Semipointed	Brooks .40 Cal. 425-Gr. Semipointed	Brooks .45 Cal. 513-Gr. Creedmoor	Brooks .45 Cal. 530-Gr. Creedmoor	Brooks .45 Cal. 544-Gr. Creedmoor

Some of Mike's favorite cast rifle bullets for shooting from 100 to 1000 yards are .30-, .40-, and .45-caliber bullets.

through these bolt actions has been modest because I've been working up cast-bullet loads for all. Conversely, my shooting passion for almost two decades has been competing in the NRA's Blackpowder Cartridge Rifle (BPCR) Silhouette game. And more recently I have joined those fellows shooting the NRA's Long Range Blackpowder Target matches. For BPCR Silhouette the metallic targets are placed at 200, 300, 385, and 500 meters. Those sound like faraway targets, but consider that the Long Range matches are fired at paper targets placed at 800, 900, and 1000 yards! The target's black bullseye is 44 inches wide, and its 10-ring is only 20 inches in diameter. Only lead-alloy bullets are allowed for both of these NRA-sanctioned shooting games. My competition rifles for these sports are one or another replica version of the Sharps Model 1874 or Remington Rolling Block. I have them in calibers such as .40-65, .45-70, .45-90, and .45-100. (I'm just getting around to working seriously with that latter cartridge.)

Hard Bullets

So let's look at how to prepare good cast-bullet loads for these two vastly different requirements. With the smokeless powder ammunition I think that the harder the bullet the better. Not only are those bullets going to be driven to fairly high velocities (I use 1600 to 1800 fps as velocity parameters for my military rifles), but they also must withstand the rigors of being cycled from a magazine, up a feedramp, and into a chamber. A softer alloy than linotype is apt to be "grabby" in such a journey and at the least will be scratched and nicked. Therefore, for my bottleneck, smokeless powder shooting only linotype alloy is used. According to Lyman's No. 48 reloading handbook, linotype will have a Brinell Hardness Number (BHN) of 22. That's about the hardest lead alloy one will commonly encounter.

Also, since a cast bullet fired from a bottleneck, smokeless powder cartridge is subjected to higher pressures, I believe they should be of gascheck design. The little gilding metal cups protect the bullet's base from being battered by gases or smokeless powder granules. For this very reason most of the cast bullet designs sold by the major bullet mold manufacturers intended for smokeless powder shooting are cut to carry gaschecks. I highly recommend the gascheck be seated with the aid of Lyman's little gascheck seating tool to ensure it is square with the bullet's base.

As for exact bullet shape, very pointed spitzer-type cast bullets seldom give good service at my desired velocity levels while semipointed and roundnose bullets shoot very well in most rifles. And here is one more item based on my experience. Whenever possible, I like my cast bullets for this sort of shooting to be a bit heavier than

the jacketed bullet weight normal for that caliber. For instance, in .30-06 150- to 180-grain jacketed bullets might be considered standard. For my .30-06 cast bullets I now prefer those from 180 to 215 grains. Admittedly without having any science to back up my opinion, I think that the heavier bullets make the relatively small smokeless powder charges burn at higher pressures and deliver better accuracy.

Want a good example of what I consider a fine smokeless powder, bottleneck cartridge cast bullet? Since I'm spending so much time working with .30-caliber military rifles, let's look at that bore size. Lyman has two versions of the same bullet; one is meant for

Mike's cast-bullet handloads are capable of fine accuracy. The .30-06 2.00-inch group is at 100 yards while the .40-65 3.5-inch group is at 300 yards.

According to the author, case neck expanding and belling dies are required for constructing accurate cast-bullet handloads.

American .30 calibers, and the other is for European-type .30 calibers. The first is No. 311299, meant to be sized about .309/.310 inch, and the latter is No. 314299, meant to be sized .313/.314 inch. Both have nominal weights of 200 grains when cast of Lyman's No. 2 alloy formula, but from linotype mine weigh 190 grains for the smaller diameter one and 195 grains for the larger. These are semipointed bullets with a long bore-riding nose and short body containing two grease grooves. Bullet No. 311299 is fine for .30-40 Krag and .30-06 while No. 314299 serves excellently in the .303 British cartridge.

BPCR and Long-Range Bullets

Now let's look at the vastly different bullets useful for BPCR Silhouette and Long Range. First off, forget the linotype alloy. Experience has proven that very hard cast bullets fired over blackpowder charges delivering velocities only in the 1150 to 1400 fps range can be accurate, but they leave excessive leading. A very hard bullet doesn't obturate to seal the bore at blackpowder pressures, and therefore gas cuts past its base and leaves melted lead plated inside the barrel. Almost universally, BPCR competitors are using blends of pure lead and pure tin in proportions of 1:20 to 1:30. The 1:30 alloy has a BHN of 9 while 1:20 alloy has a BHN of 10. I favor the 1:20 blend.

The rules for these long-range BPCR matches do not allow gas-check-type bullets, so shooters protect the bullet's bases in another way. We cut or buy wads that are placed

between the powder charge and the bullet's base. These come in many types, such as cardboard punched from ordinary tablet backing to commercial vegetable fiber and even plastic wads. In the old days I used to cut .030-inch cardboard wads myself, but since John Walters began selling his vegetable fiber wads I'll never take wad punch in hand again. Walters's wads come in all the correct sizes for blackpowder cartridge rifles and either in .030- or .060-inch thickness. I've settled on the latter for my shooting.

Most competitors shoot round-nose bullets of one form or another in the BPCR games, but at these low velocities sometimes a pointed bullet also will shoot well. Regardless, we like them heavy. In BPCR Silhouette the two most popular bore sizes are .40 and .45 caliber. For .40 caliber most shooters use bullets from 400 to 425 grains, and .45-caliber shooters like 500- to 550-grain bullets. In the NRA's Long Range matches shooters almost universally use .45-caliber rifles and prefer bullets in the 520- to 570-grain weight range.

I mentioned that my favorite .30-caliber bullets had only two grease grooves. That is opposite of what we want with our BPCR bullets. There the bullet lubricant not only serves to keep the bullet from leaving lead fouling in the bore, but it helps keep the blackpowder fouling soft. So, most of the BPCR bullets seen in competition have long bodies with four and five grease grooves.

And lastly, long-range target shooters want our bullets to be con-

sistent. Conversely, from the relatively short-range shooting I do with modern bolt actions where I like to use multiple-cavity molds to increase bullet production, I will only use single-cavity molds for long-range target competition. Most high-scoring competitors report that they weigh each and every bullet. My personal limits are that I keep my bullets within a plus/minus .3-grain spread, or a total spread of .6 grain. My 100-yard bullets for the various military rifles are not weighed at all.

As with the .30-caliber bullets, I'll detail what I think are good designs for long-range target shooting with the BPCR. Most competitors in these two games use custom lathe-bored bullet molds, with the two most popular makers being Paul Jones and Steve Brooks. I should mention that I recently discovered another maker by the name of Dave Mos.

My favorite .40-caliber BPCR Silhouette bullet is a Brooks "Turkey Killer" design of 425 grains (1:20 alloy) with pointed nose and four grease grooves. When shooting .45-caliber rifles in BPCR Silhouette I have been using Creedmoor-style roundnose bullets. These are a 513-grain bullet by Brooks or a similarly shaped 530-grain one from Mos. Both bullets have three very wide and deep grease grooves. For the 800-, 900-, and 1000-yard matches, I use another Creedmoor-style bullet that weighs 544 grains from a mold made by Steve Brooks. It is a little different than normal in that the diameter of the bullet for the top two grease grooves is the same diameter as the nose. That way it can be seated far out of the cartridge case, making more room for powder. I wanted to make a .45-70 powerful enough for the Long Range matches and by seating the bullet so far out was able to increase the blackpowder charge almost 10 grains.

Instead of sizing those bullets used for long-range competition the molds are ordered to drop the bullets at the rifle's barrel groove diameter. For instance, that is .408 inch for .40-65 and .458 inch for all .45 calibers. Then the bullets are run into lube/sizing dies slightly larger—.410 inch for the .40 caliber and .459 inch for .45 caliber. The lube is applied speedily, but the bullets are not touched by the die during the operation.

Preparing the Case

When it comes to preparing the cartridge cases for reloading, the steps are the same for 100-yard and 1000-yard ammunition. I full-length size the brass, mainly because I have more than one rifle in each caliber and want to ensure easy chambering in all of them. Next, the primer pockets are uniformed with a Sinclair Primer Pocket Uniformer. Last, the case mouths are expanded and belled with a Lyman M-Die. The M-Dies have a stepped stem. The smaller part expands the inside of the cartridge case to a proper dimension to accept cast bullets, and the larger part bells the case mouth so that the bullet's base can be started without damage. Lyman sells M-Dies for virtually all bore sizes from .22

to .50, and they are indispensable for cast-bullet shooting.

When it comes time to put powder charges into the cases, I again use two very different methods. For the modern, bottleneck .30-caliber cartridges I simply drop the desired charge from a Redding Competition BR-30 powder measure. It holds the smokeless powder charges within a couple tenths of a grain, which is fine for 100-yard shooting. For the blackpowder loads meant for long-range shooting I hand weigh each one to plus/minus .1 grain. Then I drop each of those hand-weighed powder charges down a 24-inch drop tube, taking about five seconds to trickle each one in. I don't know why, but drop-tubed blackpowder charges burn more cleanly and consistently. And I should mention that this is not a new trick; the original Sharps Rifle Co. also marketed drop tubes among its other reloading tools.

Powders

I will include only a few words about powders for all this shooting because the range of choices is just so great. There are well over 100 different smokeless powders now, and blackpowders are available from here, Germany, and Switzerland. My choice for modern, bottleneck smokeless powder cartridges is Accurate Arms XMP-5744. It burns very consistently without needing any sort of case filler and has a small enough granule size that it powder measures well. For blackpowder shooting I have settled on Swiss 1 1/2 Fg for the NRA BPCR Silhouette game. For NRA Long Range Target shooting with the .45-70 I use Swiss FFFg because it gives the cartridge extra oomph.

CAST BULLET HANDLOADS FOR 100 YARDS

Powder	Velocity		Velocity Variation	100-Yard Accuracy	
Bullet	(Type)	(Grs.)	(fps)	(fps)	(Inches)
.30-40 Krag, U.S. M1896 Springfield, 30-Inch Barrel					
Lyman No. 311299 190-gr. Semipointed XMP-5744		22.0	1789	10	2.25
.303 British, SMLE No. 4 Mark 1, 25-Inch Barrel					
Lyman No. 314299 195-gr. Semipointed XMP-5744		22.0	1728	24	3.13
.30-06, U.S. M1903A3 Springfield, 24-Inch Barrel					
Lyman No. 311299 190-gr. Semipointed XMP-5744		25.0	1785	31	2.08

NOTES: Accuracy is the average of three five-shot groups fired from a sandbag benchrest at 100 yards. Velocity is the average of five rounds measured six feet from the guns' muzzles.

LONG-RANGE CAST BULLET HANDLOADS

Powder	Velocity		Velocity Variation	300-Yard Accuracy	
Bullet	(Type)	(Grs.)	(fps)	(fps)	(Inches)
.40-65 Lone Star Rolling Block, 32-Inch Barrel					
Brooks 425-gr. Semipointed Swiss 1½ Fg		57.0	1204	9	3.42
.45-70 C. Sharps Arms Model 1874, 32-Inch Barrel					
Brooks 513-gr. Creedmoor Swiss 1½ Fg		70.0	1212	13	4.33
Mos 530-gr. Creedmoor Swiss 1½ Fg		67.0	1167	15	4.08
Brooks 544-gr. Creedmoor Swiss FFFg		68.0	1254	10	4.21
.45-90 Shiloh Model 1874, 30-Inch Barrel					
Mos 530-gr. Creedmoor Swiss 1½ Fg		78.0	1246	18	4.50
Brooks 544-gr. Creedmoor Swiss 1½ Fg		75.0	1208	13	3.88

NOTES: Accuracy is the average of three five-shot groups fired from a sandbag benchrest at 300 yards. Velocity is the average of 10 rounds measured six feet from the guns' muzzles.

When firing the .45-90 cartridge in that game I return to Swiss 1 1/2 Fg.

Bullet Seating

Now we get to the bullet seating step. For my modern bottleneck cartridges the bullet is seated in the normal manner in a standard seating die with all grease grooves covered, and then I apply a rather heavy crimp. That is to ensure the bullet stays in place during the sometimes rough travel from military rifle magazine into chamber. For my long-range blackpowder match ammunition each bullet is seated with the aid of a Redding micrometer adjustable Competition Seating Die. The spring-loaded inner sleeve of that die helps ensure the alignment of bullet to cartridge case. Before using these rounds in competition, I further check them with a Sinclair concentricity gauge. I find that my rounds seldom have more than .001 inch of run out.

Unlike with the modern bottleneck smokeless powder cartridges where I let the bullet's crimping groove dictate the seating depth of the bullet, with the blackpowder match rounds I have invested considerable experimentation to determine seating depth. For instance, my Lone Star Rolling Block and Shiloh Sharps Model 1874 .40-65s give best groups with the 425-grain Brooks Turkey Killer bullet to be seated with one grease groove exposed. My custom Remington Rolling Block and C. Sharps Arms Model 1874 .45-70s and my Shiloh Model 1874 Sharps .45-90 like the Brooks and Mos Postell bullets to be seated with all grease grooves covered. That C. Sharps Arms Model 1874 .45-70 is one I have won some awards with (but nary a first place yet!) in the 800-, 900-, and 1000-yard events. And I did the shooting with the Brooks 544-grain Creedmoor seated with two full grease grooves exposed.

After all is said and done, just how well does my 100- to 1000-yard ammunition shoot? I've enclosed some of my favorite loads in the accompanying chart, but I'll give these details. No major problem has been encountered in getting my 1903 Springfield .30-06s or the U.S. Krag .30-40 to give groups from 1 1/2 to 2 MOA at 100 yards. The British SMLE No. 4 Mark 1 .303 and the Model 1917 Enfields are more like 2 to 3 MOA shooters.

I won't compete with one of my BPCR Long Range rifles unless it will deliver groups of about 1 1/2 MOA at 300 yards. And I've managed to shoot myself into the Master Class in both of those very difficult shooting sports.

Perhaps I was lucky in my early years in that I was forced to go the cast-bullet route in my reloading endeavors. It made me appreciate that species of projectile and has caused me to get the very most enjoyment out of handloading.

ACCURACY FACT–BULLET SEATING DEPTH

BY LAYNE SIMPSON

As a rule, most rifles will shoot more accurately when the bullets in handloads are seated out close to or sometimes even against the rifling. But like many rules this one is not carved in granite. I recently had a 9 1/2-pound big-game rifle built in a .300 Magnum wildcat chambering that is commonly used for 1000-yard benchrest competition. The cartridge burns more than 100 grains of H5010 while launching a 180-grain bullet at more than 3400 fps. The gunsmith's chamber reamer had been ground to cut a long chamber throat for use with the Sierra 250-grain MatchKing in single-shot target rifles. When lighter hunting bullets are seated to an overall cartridge length compatible with the magazine in my rifle, the bullet has to leap through a great deal of space before engaging the rifling, yet this rifle consistently keeps three Nosler 180-grain Ballistic Tips inside a half-inch at 100 yards.

Quite often a rifle with a relatively long chamber throat will shoot more accurately with heavier bullets than with the lightweights. I usually find flatbase bullets to be more accurate than boattail bullets in a long-throated chamber. I suspect this is because the longer bearing surface of a heavy flatbase bullet is better at resisting any slight misalignment as it leaps from case to rifling. On average a long-throated rifle will shoot more accurately with maximum or near-maximum loads than with lighter loads. Some rifles with extremely long chamber throats will not shoot anything they are fed with decent accuracy, but there are plenty of exceptions. The owner of such a rifle should not immediately abandon all hope of shooting tiny groups just because its magazine won't allow bullets to be seated out close to the rifling. You'll never know until you try.

How to Shoot

BY DAVID M. FORTIER

HIGH

High Power competition has evolved down through the decades. Targets have changed and rifles have improved, but the goal remains the same. High Power competition is intended to teach, improve, and refine the marksmanship skills of riflemen—military and civilian. Skills that someday may be required on the battlefield.

This is accomplished through a course of fire designed to hone the fundamentals of shooting. Each match is divided into multiple stages of one or more strings. Each stage is designed to develop and test the rifleman, against the clock, to achieve a particular shooting position (standing, sitting or kneeling, or prone), proper sight and body alignment with the target, trigger control, and breathing. The stages are also designed to force him to learn how to make smooth reloads and correct sight adjustments

and read environmental conditions. The result is a rifleman with the foundational skills that allow him to effectively wield an iron-sighted rifle on static targets out to 600 yards.

The process of becoming truly proficient with a rifle is not a simple one. It takes a conscious decision followed by hard work, sacrifice, and dedication. More importantly, it takes strength of character to drive on when training becomes more like a chore than like

POWER

If you are thinking about trying High Power rifle competition, these simple tips will help improve your scores.

Although the two taped sighters here were perfect Xs, the 10 shots for record dropped low, probably due to a slight change in position.

fun. I wish I could tell you everything you need to know to become an expert rifleman on these few pages. Unfortunately that's not realistic. What I can do is share information gleaned from my own experiences as well as those of Shawn McKenna, one of the best Service Rifle shooters in our great country.

1. Believe in Yourself

The place to start is with your mental attitude. It is your most important tool. It needs to be positive, focused on the task at hand, and open to constructive criticism. There is no room for the phrase, "I can't." Running a rifle is not brain surgery, and you can learn to be a competent marksman if you are willing to put in the work. Just because you have never shot past 100 or 200 yards does not mean you can't learn how to hit at extended distances. You can. Understand that it's fear of failure that keeps most people from even trying. But failure is simply part of the cycle of life. The trick is to learn from your mistakes and continue to improve.

Also, don't allow yourself to be intimidated by stages of fire, other shooters, or conditions. Understand that it is normal to be nervous in

competition, especially when you first start. Often shooters are intimidated by certain courses of fire, usually offhand. Why? Well, shooting offhand is hard. Just understand that it's equally hard for everyone. Just focus on shooting the stage one shot at a time. And don't be intimidated by other "big name" shooters. They are deserving of respect, but they

are only flesh and blood—just like you. Rather than being intimidated by them, analyze how they do things in order to improve your own performance. You may feel like you're the only person on the line who is nervously waiting for the targets to appear, but you aren't. You have to harness that energy and refocus it in a positive manner.

Very important is how you react to

Champion High Power shooter Shawn McKenna shows how he sets up his gear. Note how both his spotting scope and stool are within easy reach.

have to stretch, contort, or move to look through it, then you do not have it placed optimally. Placing your spotting scope poorly will only fatigue you and make life more difficult than it has to be. Your stool should be placed where it and its contents are within easy reach. Then lay out any items you will need (ammunition, magazines, logbook, timer, pen, sweat rag, water) so you can easily grab whatever you need. This all sounds very simple and straightforward, but many shooters set up their gear in such a way that makes their time competing more difficult.

3. Build a Solid Shooting Position

It's extremely important to be able to quickly find your natural point of aim on varying types of terrain and build a solid position. Shooting is about applying and executing the basics on command, and being able to find your natural point of aim is a fundamental skill. Another is building a solid position. With a solid position, the rapid-fire stages should be a gimme if you're shooting a "mousegun." A solid position is mandatory to do well with an M14 in the rapids. How do you know if you have a solid position? When in position your breathing should cause the front sight to track vertically through the black. Take some deep breaths and force all the air out and watch what the front sight does. Then fire a round and watch what the front sight does. The front sight should track vertically straight up through recoil and then return. If it doesn't, something is wrong and you need to adjust your position. If you have a solid position and throw a shot wide, it's a breakdown of the other fundamentals.

4. Use Enough Sling Tension

It's common to see shooters who do not understand the basic principle of how a loop sling functions, and they fail to adjust their sling tight enough, negating its usefulness. In order for a loop sling to be truly effective it

a botched shot. It's going to happen, and you need to be able to deal with it mentally so that it doesn't have a negative effect on the rest of your shooting. When you botch a shot, you have to accept it, then move on and forget about it. Concentrate only on the shot you are making, not the six you just pounded out. The idea is to shoot the match one round at a time, trying to make each one a 10.

And don't make the mistake of trying to keep score in your head. Worrying about your score will only distract you. Don't do it. Your job is to shoot, so concentrate on that and let the score take care of itself at the end of the match.

2. Set Up Gear Properly

It's important to be prepared when you move to the line so you can concentrate on shooting, instead of where you put your gear. When you set up on the line, place your spotting scope at a height and angle so you can easily look through it without coming out of position. When shooting prone you should be able to look through your spotting scope by simply lifting your head slightly off your stock. If you

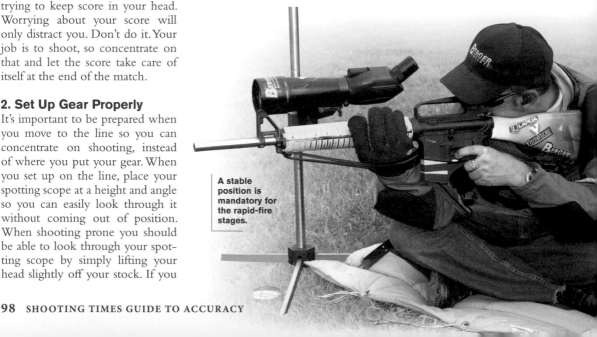

A stable position is mandatory for the rapid-fire stages.

Many shooters, but not this one, don't apply enough tension to their loop sling.

needs to be extremely tight, especially if you're shooting an M14. How tight? You should have to physically push the butt of the rifle forward in order to get it into your shoulder. This amount of sling tension is not comfortable, but it's normal. For an idea on the amount of sling tension I am talking about, let me just comment that it is not uncommon for shooters to break leather military M1907 loop slings or to rip sling swivels out of forends. But understand, you are only going to be in position in the rapids for maybe 50 or 60 seconds. When shooting slow-fire prone I loosen my sling up one notch from my rapid-fire prone setting. Despite this it's not uncommon for me to lose sensation in my arm midway through a 20-shot slow-fire string.

A Brief History of High Power Competition

Informal competition shooting has always been an important part of American culture. In the early 1700s frontiersmen gathered to test their skills against one another in "rifle frolics." Shooting offhand or from a rest, they put their rifles, and themselves, to the test competing for prizes such as food. More formalized competition shooting gradually took hold after the introduction of the percussion lock. It was the Civil War, though, that had the greatest long-term impact on competitive shooting.

The dismal marksmanship exhibited by Union soldiers due to a lack of systematic training led directly to the foundation of the National Rifle Association in 1871. This organization was destined to play a key role in solidly establishing formal competition shooting in the United States. Founded by former officers of the Union Army, as well as the state guards, the NRA's goal was to improve the marksmanship level of the military through "scientific" training. This stands in stark contrast to the very rudimentary firearms familiarization normally given to troops during that time.

Matches began at the Creedmoor range on Long Island in October 1873. From very humble beginnings the competitive shooting sports began to slowly grow. Then in 1903, while President Theodore Roosevelt was in office, Congress created the National Board for the Promotion of Rifle Practice. This established the National Rifle and Pistol Matches and also provided funding for the transport of military personnel to such matches. The first National Matches were held at Fort Riley in Kansas in 1904. They were subsequently moved to Camp Perry in Ohio in 1907 where they became an annual event.

Today most individual and team matches use the 50-shot NRA National Match Course (NMC), 80-shot NRA Regional Match Course (RMC), or CMP Service Rifle equivalent. These events are referred to as "across the course" matches because they are shot at a variety of distances from the target. Each match, with the exception of the CMP's three-stage President's Match, is comprised of four different stages of fire.

The 50-shot NRA NMC is as follows: The first stage is shot slow-fire offhand at 200 yards. Here you have 10 minutes to fire 10 rounds, with cartridges loaded one at a time. After each shot the target is pulled and the location of the hit, as well as its value, is marked before being run back up. Offhand is followed by a rapid-fire sitting (or kneeling, the choice is up to the competitor) stage shot at the same distance. During this stage you start from the standing position and have 60 seconds to drop to a sitting position and fire 10 rounds. After the first two rounds are fired a mandatory reload is required, followed by firing the last eight rounds.

Next, shooters move back to the 300-yard line for rapid-fire prone. Once again, shooters start from standing, then drop to the prone position and fire 10 rounds in 70 seconds. Again, a mandatory reload after two rounds is required. At both 200 and 300 yards the bullseye targets feature a 7-inch 10-ring and a 3-inch X-ring. For the last stage shooters carry their gear all the way back to the 600-yard line for slow-fire prone. During this final stage you have 20 minutes to fire 20 rounds with rounds loaded one at a time. As during the offhand stage, the targets are pulled and scored after each shot. The 600-yard target features a 12-inch 10-ring and a 6-inch X-ring. The 80-shot NRA Regional Match Course is identical to this, except rounds fired during the first three stages are doubled, from 10 to 20. ∎

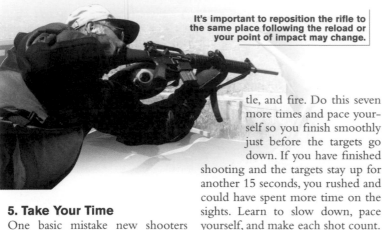

It's important to reposition the rifle to the same place following the reload or your point of impact may change.

5. Take Your Time

One basic mistake new shooters make is rushing through the rapid-fire shots. There is more than enough time; don't rush. When the targets rise, drop down and get into a solid position. Take the time here to ensure everything is right. Then inhale and exhale, wait for the front sight to stabilize, and fire. Repeat this sequence and then perform a smooth reload. It's very important to get the rifle back into the exact same position following the reload. After the reload, again inhale and exhale, wait for the front sight to set-tle, and fire. Do this seven more times and pace yourself so you finish smoothly just before the targets go down. If you have finished shooting and the targets stay up for another 15 seconds, you rushed and could have spent more time on the sights. Learn to slow down, pace yourself, and make each shot count.

6. Know When to Log Data and When to Shoot

I believe every shooter should own and use a logbook. But you have to know when to log information and when to shoot. If you're on the 600-yard line, just had your third 10 come up, and the wind hasn't changed, then forget about the logbook. Take advantage of the conditions and get rounds downrange. In this regard I am a fairly fast shooter on slow-fire stages. If the conditions are good and I am shooting well, I will break my shot right after the target comes back up.

7. The Wind Is Not Your Enemy

Many shooters fear the wind. Don't have that attitude; the wind is not your enemy. Can the wind be difficult to shoot in? Without a doubt. However, instead of fearing it, accept the challenge of learning to understand it. Then seek out the wisdom of those who can help you to learn how to read and adjust for it.

8. It's Not about the Gear

Becoming proficient with a rifle is not about the gear. It's about you and the work and effort you are willing to put in to it. Don't fall down the rabbit hole of throwing money at a problem. You don't need a fancy, leather shooting jacket, tricked-out Tubb 2000, and every shooting widget under the sun to become proficient with a rifle. A simple field jacket, winter glove, M1 web sling, and CMP Garand with some decent ammo will get you started. Will quality gear make a difference? Of course. But there comes a point when High Power ceases to be a useful training aid for learning practical marksmanship skills and simply becomes a pursuit unto itself. You have to decide what you want out of this sport.

9. Seek Out Wisdom

Let me be very blunt here: You will not get very far if you try to do everything on your own. Quality instruction, more than anything else, will help to you quickly and dramatically improve your skills. There are plenty of top shooters around the country who are more than happy to share their knowledge. So seek their counsel. Remember, "iron sharpeneth iron." With each passing year the number of true riflemen left in this country dwindles. Only you can do something to change this. Become a rifleman yourself—and help a friend to become one, too.

Nothing will improve your shooting as much as quality instruction and good coaching.

PART IV
OTHER FIREARMS

1911s

FOR BULLSEYE

A LOOK INSIDE

In order to make the most accurate and the most reliable 1911s going, custom gunsmiths pull out all the stops when building pistols for Bullseye competition.

BY REID COFFIELD

OFFICIAL

6

8

9

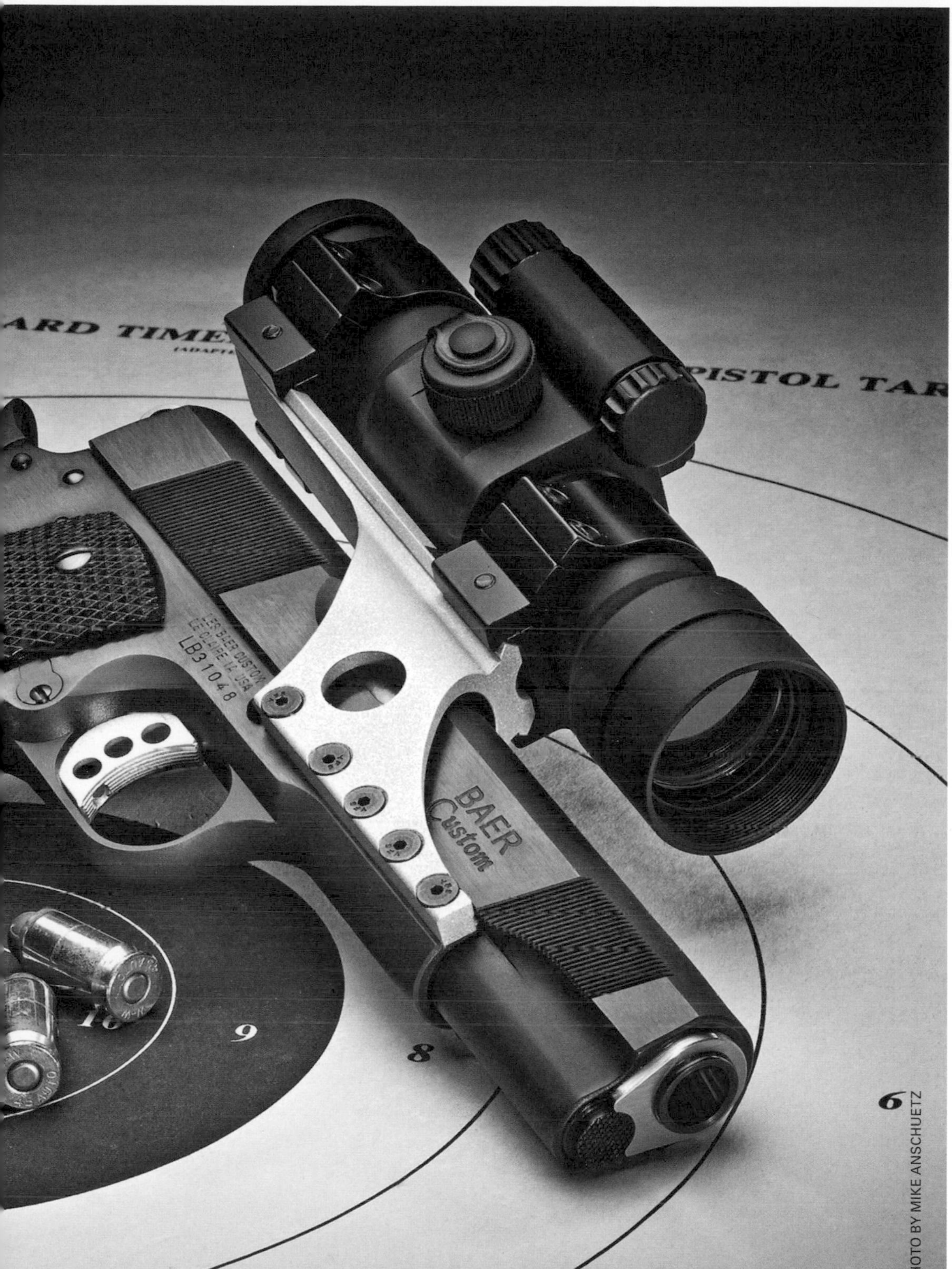

PHOTO BY MIKE ANSCHUETZ

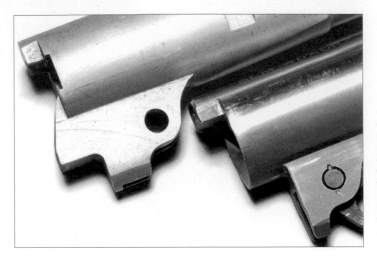

◀ A ramped, or supported, barrel (left) requires careful custom fitting to the frame, but it normally provides better feeding than a conventional barrel (right).

The Model 1911 Auto Pistol is justifiably considered by many to be the most popular handgun in the United States. Countless gun companies have produced variations of the venerable Colt Model 1911. Even Colt's historic firearms rival, Smith & Wesson, has gotten on board and offers 1911s. Remington, after a 94-year hiatus from producing 1911s, now has a couple of 1911s in its line. And, finally, even Ruger now offers 1911s! In addition, since World War II, custom gunsmiths have done amazing things with this platform, producing extremely accurate and reliable handguns for many different uses. Whether it's a home-defense gun, a plinker, a custom combat handgun, or a Bullseye gun accurate enough to win the National Championship at Camp Perry, there's a 1911 available to you, and they are all based on the time-tested and proven John M. Browning design.

With this huge number of 1911s on the market and with so many different variations, it can get darn confusing. After all, when you look at 1911s and get beyond the finish, sights, and a few external features, they tend to look alike. But even though they look very similar, there's often a huge difference in price, especially between factory and custom guns. It would make anyone wonder why and what the real differences are.

For example, let's take a look at some of the major differences between a precision, custom-made 1911 set up for use with wadcutter ammo for serious Bullseye competition and a standard 1911 intended for general use with ball ammo. Before I get into the mechanical details, I'd like to point out some major changes in how most 1911s are made today.

The vast majority of U.S. 1911 manufacturers now use extremely sophisticated computer controlled and guided machines to fabricate the various components. This is in sharp contrast to the normal situation not all that many years ago.

Just a few years back, I remember going into a firearms manufacturing plant and seeing row after row of milling machines, each operated by one individual, all making the same part. Granted, all those fellows working on those individual machines might have been extremely skilled and knowledgeable machinists, but, still, at the end of the day, those 30 or 50 guys were going to have produced parts that were each just a bit different from all the rest. No two of them were exactly alike. It just wasn't humanly possible to make them all perfectly identical. Not only did you have to deal with the variations and individual accuracy tolerances of the 30 to 50 machines, but also you had to deal with the differences in the guys running them.

"Joe" might've had a rough night and just didn't get enough sleep. "Sam" might've been worrying about his kids. And "Pete" could've been daydreaming about a hunting trip. Any of those things could make those fellows just a little less attentive to what they were doing. Their work could still have been acceptable, but the tolerances for "acceptable" were necessarily fairly large if the manufacturer wanted to get any reasonable amount of production. This led to a lot of necessary handfitting of parts that

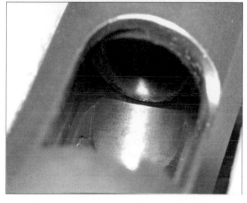

▲A customized 1911 with ramped barrel also generally has a polished feedramp (top) as opposed to a standard two-part feedramp (bottom) The two-part feedramp works fine with ball ammo, but it can, and often will, fail to feed wadcutters or hollowpoints.

otherwise might or might not go together all that well. Or, at the other end of the spectrum, it meant that the parts went together very easily but were really loose or sloppy. Since handfitting takes time and resources, which means extra expense for the manufacturer, the tendency was naturally to make the parts that would not require handwork during assembly. And, yes, that meant the fit of the guns tended to be more or less sloppy.

The introduction of computer-controlled equipment had a dramatic effect on modern firearms producers and led to major changes. Instead of 30 to 50 milling machines, you now might find

only three or four large computer-controlled machining centers. These incredible machines are often designed to do multiple operations and thus replace a number of older manual machines. In addition, being computer controlled, these machines never get tired, never get sleepy, never worry about the kids, never daydream about how it's gonna spend its day off. It does the same procedure time after time, quickly, and with more consistent precision than any human.

These amazing machines can even be set up to compensate for wear on the cutters, reamers, and drills used to make the parts. They can make parts that are held to tolerances to within one ten-thousandth of an inch—or even greater precision! They can often be programmed to shut down and alert the operator if there's a problem or if the part is not made to spec. All of this enables the manufacturer to make the parts to greater consistent uniformity and to extraordinarily tight or close tolerances, yet still require little or no expensive and time-consuming handfitting.

One of the standard criticisms of many modern guns is that they don't have the handwork found on older guns. Well, they don't necessarily need it! The parts fit from the get-go and don't have to be filed, stoned, or beat into place to work. The reality is that for the most part, modern handguns—in this case normal, average production 1911s in the middle price range—are now

being produced with tighter tolerances and better fitting parts than at any time in the past. Sure, even in the past, custom, handfit, commercial, target-grade 1911s were darn good, but those were unique and special handguns. They weren't the typical average 1911.

Comparing a factory-grade 1911 made during World War II to a standard, medium-priced, no-frills 1911 made today by any of the major manufacturers is like comparing apples to oranges. They are truly two different guns, if for no other reasons than the manufacturing techniques used and the tolerances allowed. The typical newer gun is consistently more accurate and better made by a huge margin.

Perhaps a more significant comparison is between today's factory guns and currently produced custom guns. Hold on a minute, you say. Haven't those advances in technology and firearms production made the differences in quality and accuracy much smaller? Didn't you just say that today's 1911s are tighter and better made than ever? Why pay more when that off-the-shelf gun will do the same job? Aren't you just paying big bucks for a name or cosmetics?

Granted, while the newer factory 1911s are better than ever, there's still room for the custom 1911. While tolerances are tighter and many custom options and accessories of years ago are now standard, there are still significant differences between the two.

The Bullseye Difference

The heart of any firearm is the barrel, and that's a good place to begin. The standard factory-produced gun usually has a pretty good barrel. It's sure better than the typical barrel used on most guns years ago, but it's not as good as a premium barrel used by a good custom gunmaker. Remember, factory guns have to compete with lots of other factory guns, and price is critical. Consequently, barrels that are more often than not subcontracted to other suppliers are one of the places where the gun factory bean counters will cut costs. Don't get me wrong; you'll generally get a good serviceable barrel, but it won't be as good as the barrel you'll get on a custom gun. You'll be paying more for that custom gun barrel, and more often than not, you'll get what you pay for.

There are other points to consider. Many custom pistolsmiths will set up their 1911s with ramped barrels, or what is sometimes referred to as supported barrels. These are barrels made with an integral feedramp, and this requires extra work in cutting the frame for the ramp, which extends below the chamber, as well as a good bit of special handfitting. The factory-produced guns are made with traditional nonramped barrels with the feedramp built into the frame. That works, but it will never feed as well or as reliably with wadcutter or hollowpoint ammunition. The advantage to the manufacturer with the nonramped barrel is that it's less expensive and makes for faster production.

It's also important to be aware that custom pistolsmiths will spend many hours handfitting the barrel to the frame and the slide. They don't depend just on the close tolerances of the individual parts. This, more than anything else, makes the difference in the accuracy of the handgun. Keep in mind that almost all custom pistolsmiths will guarantee a high degree of accuracy with their handguns. They'll normally specify how big a group your gun will shoot at 25 and 50 yards, and it'll be small! How small? About 2.5 inches or less at 50 yards. The big gun manufacturers will seldom provide accuracy information—or even tell you what their accuracy acceptance criteria are. It's reasonably good and will normally meet the needs of most of their customers, but it's far below what you can expect with a good custom 1911.

By the way, many custom 1911 pistolsmiths will even go so far as to test-fire their barrels before they are used in building a pistol. A special fixture is used to allow the barrel to be tested for accuracy. This is done to ensure the gun will shoot to an extremely high level of accuracy once it's completed. The pistolsmith is not going to be surprised by a "lemon" after he spends hours putting the gun together. He knows before he starts his gun will be a supe-

◀ The differences between a custom extractor (left) and a mass-produced extractor (right) are easily noticed. The custom extractor will be handfitted to a slide, whereas the factory extractor will drop in with no special fitting.

rior shooter. That sort of thing never happens with the average factory gun, and that's one reason why some factory guns shoot fairly well and others not so well.

You'll find similar situations when you look at the other internal components. An extractor looks deceptively simple. It's just a rod with a hook on the end of it designed to jerk the fired case out of the chamber, right? Well, there's a lot more to it than that. The extractor on a custom 1911 will be set up so that there's minimal distance between the inside of the extractor hook and the breechface of the slide. This helps to ensure consistent and reliable extraction and proper positioning of the cartridge as it's stripped from the magazine and fed into the chamber. On a custom gun the builder is concerned not just with reliable functioning but with every detail of how that part affects the loaded, as well as the fired, cartridge.

As with the barrel and other parts, a custom gunmaker will tend to use a higher quality

▲ **Custom pistolsmiths also spend a lot of time making sure the slide's breechface is silky smooth and that its relationship to the extractor is correct for optimal functioning.**

extractor. It'll be made from better materials and to tighter tolerances. And, most importantly, it'll be handfitted in the slide and adjusted to exert a specific amount of tension on the cartridge rim. You won't find that attention to detail on the typical factory gun.

I mentioned the slide breechface relative to the extractor. Part of the fitting of the slide and barrel entails a lot of detail work on the slide. The breechface on a custom gun will be polished to give it a super-smooth surface. Some custom gunsmiths will even give the breechface a mirror polish. It isn't just for looks. As the loaded round is stripped from the magazine and the rim slips under the extractor, the base of the cartridge case must slide up the breechface as the round is chambered. A highly polished breechface makes this much easier and more reliable. That's just one more feature of a custom gun. The typical factory gun seldom has any work done on the breechface. It's used pretty much just as it comes off the production machine.

The trigger is another good example of the differences you'll see in custom and standard production guns. The trigger on a custom gun not only will tend to be of higher quality, but also it'll generally have a greater degree of adjustment. For example, it's pretty much standard on a custom 1911 for the trigger to be easily adjustable for overtravel. Of course, it'll be handfitted to the frame to eliminate even the slightest degree of unnecessary movement.

It's basically the same story with all the other parts. The custom gunmaker will generally use much higher quality parts made of better materials and to tighter tolerances. He'll then carefully handfit those parts to the frame and slide. This means it takes more time for him to build a gun, and he has a lot more money tied up in components and materials.

If you're getting the idea that custom pistolsmiths are a bit compulsive when it comes to seemingly insignificant details, you're right. As many of my pistolsmith friends will admit, they're indeed a bit on the strange side. However, it's that total focus and attention to the smallest detail that makes a really good custom 1911 so darn great.

The secret of better accuracy and superior performance is really not that much of a secret. It's just plain old-fashioned attention to detail, even what you might think is the smallest and least significant detail. In addition, accuracy requires the use of superior components. Of course, that all adds up to more cost, and that's where the gun manufacturers are at a disadvantage. They have to keep their costs down in order to be competitive. The custom pistolsmith, on the other hand, has a more limited market, but those customers are willing to pay more for their guns. Those customers recognize and understand they'll be getting more value for their dollar in terms of performance, accuracy, and reliability.

Years ago, a good friend of mine and I were attending a major gun show, and we had an opportunity to look at a couple of Model 1911s made by one of the premier custom pistolsmiths in the nation. As we looked them over, my friend compared them to a fine Swiss watch. That was a good comparison—then and now. Even though I can only afford a Timex, I can sure appreciate a nice Rolex!

DIY HEART TRANSPLANT
IMPROVE YOUR 1911'S ACCURACY WITH A NEW BARREL

A lot of pistol modifications produce no tangible benefits. A barrel upgrade is one exception, and better accuracy is the result.

By Charles E. Petty

I doubt that many would argue that the 1911 pistol is the single-hottest-selling handgun on the market today. They are available from a host of sources, both foreign and domestic, and the guns we can get today are a far cry from those we had when Colt had the monopoly.

It is so rare as to be remarkable if a new 1911 pistol—regardless of who made it—does not feed and function right out of the box, and most shoot far better than the 5- to 6-inch groups of old.

Almost everyone likes to put a personal touch on their guns, but most of the things we used to do, such as installing sights and beavertail safeties, are done for us already thanks to Kimber and Springfield. When Kimber introduced its Custom Target with a factory-installed beavertail, extended thumb safety, and good sights, the company really revitalized the 1911 market, but it also took away some fun from the home gunsmith and money from the professional. Today, guns of the

pattern, such as the Loaded Springfield featured in this report, don't leave much to be desired.

But there are two things we hear shooters still complain about: accuracy and the trigger. Both are fairly easy to remedy unless the accuracy problem arises from the shooter flinching or jerking the trigger. No gunsmith can fix those issues, and if people won't believe that it's their fault, even the best coach can't fix 'em either. I guess accuracy means different things to different peo-

ple, but my view is based on the absolute certainty that we will never have an absolute answer. The choice of ammunition alone can turn pig's ears into silk purses or gilt carriages into pumpkins.

There is also a lot of mythology associated with improving accuracy in the 1911 that is either marginal or downright fraudulent. Things like group grippers, guide rods, links, bushings, and duct tape are all claimed to improve accuracy. Some do for a while, but unless the major accuracy issues are addressed in some permanent form, more often than not, it's a waste of time and money. The most important thing of all is that the barrel returns to the same place after every shot. If it does, rather pedestrian barrels will shoot well, and good ones will shine. There are three points to ponder.

The single, most important is the fit of the bottom barrel lugs to the slide-stop pin. Of lesser importance are the fit of the headspace extension on the barrel to the slide, and the barrel bushing-to-slide fit.

One of the myths is that if you put in a tight bushing, things will get better. Of course, if it's too tight, the gun won't work at all; if it is really binding, it can break stuff. But the bushing by itself is really only a small part of the story.

Another fallacy is that tightening the slide does wonders. Actually this is probably the least important part because if the barrel is properly fitted, it will take up much of the slide play. The only time slide fit is a big deal is in the few microseconds that the bullet is going down the barrel. As long as the barrel is locked up and stays that way long enough for the bullet to get gone, the rest doesn't matter. That time is provided by the flats on the bottom barrel lugs, which allow the barrel to move to the rear about 0.020 inch before it begins to unlock—ample time for the bullet to leave. The unlocking is done by the barrel link, whose only purpose in life is to pull the barrel down out of battery and help get it started upward on the return.

One question that comes up all the time is who makes the best barrels. I have been able to test quite a few in a fixture that allows only the barrel to be tested independent of the gun. I have concluded that there really is not very much difference between a World War II GI barrel and one of today's finest match barrels. I shot 13 different barrels and fired five 10-shot groups from each at 50 yards. The ammo was Federal Gold Medal 185-grain .45 ACP, and the accuracy range was from a smallest average of 1.36 inches to a largest of 1.99 inches. There was a difference of 0.28 inch in the averages of the top nine barrels. With things that close, it's hard to crown a winner with any degree of statistical accuracy.

I'm pretty sure that there is a barrel spirit out there somewhere who, like the Gremlins of flying lore, exists just to confound us poor shooters by making two seemingly identical barrels shoot as if they were mortal enemies—one good, one bad. I've tested barrels made by the most common rifling processes—button, broach, and ECM (electro-chemical machining)—and can detect no

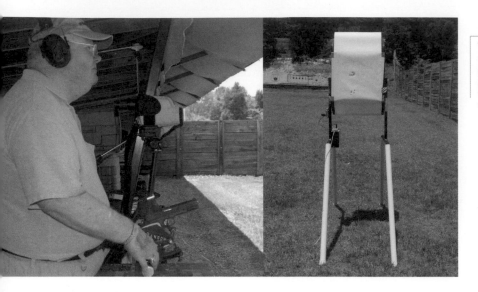

The author modified a manually operated target system with a battery powered gear motor to advance the paper. A 100-yard spool of phone wire allows the paper to be advanced with a button at the firing line.

superior manufacturing method. There surely must be differences attributable to chambering methods and rifling design, but those typically escape the understanding of ordinary folks like me.

In a very real way we have witnessed a revolution in the 1911 pistol that has been brought about by modern manufacturing capabilities that did not exist even a few years ago. Of course, I'm talking about CNC machining that can do with one or two machines almost all the work needed to make a 1911. This has given us more accurate and reliable pistols than we've ever seen before.

For the purpose of this report, I requested one of Springfield Armory's new Loaded 1911A1 .45 ACP pistols. The venerable 1911 is simply selling like hotcakes, and this model has most of the amenities everyone wants in a package that is ready to go when you open the box. Among them are beavertail, ambi safety, beveled mag well, forward slide serrations, Novak-style night sights, and two-piece recoil spring guide rod. Those are nice, but the really cool part is how well they are put together.

A sharp file helps keep straight lines. When filing the headspace extension, one crooked stroke can ruin a barrel.

As the hood is fitted, you need to check frequently to make sure everything is straight. The easiest way is to hold it up to the light.

The slide-to-frame fit would make some custom 'smiths jealous because there is a virtually imaginary bit of play, and it moves freely with no hint of binding. The barrel headspace extension mates with the slide with no light visible, and the bottom barrel lugs and slide-stop pin kiss gently when the barrel locks up. All of these are highly desirable factors made possible by the state-of-the-art manufacturing facilities at Springfield's South American supplier.

The modern equipment has made it possible to refine dimensions and reduce tolerances throughout the process. Springfield's ace gunsmith, David Williams, explained that several years ago they began to work on these elements, and the improvements are obvious. There was nothing wrong with earlier Loaded guns, but these are better.

My plan was to get a good, quality stock gun, test it, and then see what I could do to improve it, first with a drop-in match barrel and then with a barrel that required fitting. Did my new Loaded 1911 really need a heart transplant? For most purposes, the shooting results prove that it

really didn't. But it certainly gave me a nice, clean starting point to show you how you can transform your old 1911 into a real shooter.

With advice from Larry Weeks at Brownells, I chose the Nowlin Pre-fit match barrel. Based on my experience, I picked the Kart Easy Fit barrel. Springfield uses hammer-forged barrels on the Loaded guns. Nowlin barrels are rifled using the ECM process, and Kart's barrels are a combination of broach and button rifling.

The Nowlin barrel truly did drop in and was ready to go with no fuss at all. When I held the slide up to the light, there was virtually no daylight showing around the hood, and the barrel went into and out of battery with no drag. At the other end, the bushing supplied with the Nowlin barrel was a good fit on the barrel and was even slightly snug in the slide. A bushing wrench was helpful, although you could turn it with finger pressure if you don't mind a little pain.

My experience with Kart barrels has been overwhelmingly positive, and the "easy fit" makes it possible to get a hard-fit barrel without hav-

ing to cut the bottom barrel lugs—which is by far the most challenging part of a gunsmith-fit barrel installation. What Kart has done is build in a pair of "pads" inside the rearmost top lug, and by gradually filing these down until the barrel locks up, you can get the same accuracy outcome with considerably less work.

In any gunsmith fit, the first step is to cut the back and sides of the hood (headspace extension) so it will fit the slot in the slide. The ideal is for the barrel to move freely up and down in the slide but leave no space visible around the hood when you hold it up to the light. Kart's instructions permit a small clearance on the side, but I still prefer no daylight.

Once the sides are cut properly, the end of the hood is filed until the barrel can begin to go up into the slide. At this point, the fitting pads will prevent the barrel from locking up, and they must be evenly cut down until the barrel locks up. Kart also offers a tool kit for the Easy Fit barrels that includes a work bushing, a barrel-locating block (to be sure the lugs are not canted to one side or the other), and a fine file with

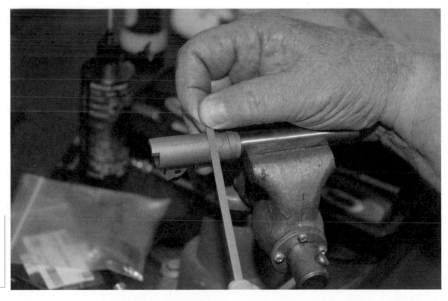

The two pads within the top locking lugs of the Kart barrel require careful fitting to make sure it locks up correctly. A file ground specifically for this job by Kart aids in the process.

safe edges that will just fit into the top barrel lugs so you can file down the contact pads.

A variation of this fitting method has been around for awhile either in the form of silver soldering a pressure pad inside the slide or by putting a couple of spots of weld inside the top barrel lugs. Kart estimates that it takes about an hour to do the job, and I'd say that is pretty close. It took me a bit longer because I was being really careful, and since the whole process involves cutting just a little with the file and trying it, patience is the best virtue one can have.

Basically there are three steps: fit the hood, fit the pads, and then fit the bushing. The first two are done with the work bushing in the kit, or you can use a loose GI bushing if you prefer. The final step is the new bushing.

The fit of barrel to bushing is done at the factory, but we have to make it fit the slide. On most guns this will mean that we have to remove some metal from the outside diameter, or skirt, of the bushing, carefully avoiding the locking lug that engages inside the slide.

When I began, it would not even start to go into the Springfield slide. This is one of those places where it is easy to take off too much. The easiest way is to use a belt sander or drill press where you can spin the bushing and take just a little at a time using either a file or Emery cloth. I made a tool for this purpose years ago, but you could easily whittle down a piece of wooden dowel for the job. It can also be done with a hand file. The secret to filing a round surface is to start with the file handle up at a high angle and rock it down as you push forward. That way it is possible to go around the circumference of the bushing in a series of strokes, rotating the bushing each time in the vise.

As I fitted the hood, my calipers showed that the sides were fine as they were, so I slowly began working on the back. It is difficult to cut a straight line with a file because of a tendency to tip it one way or another, so my policy is to make a very gentle cut to see that things are straight and keep doing that until the barrel begins to go up into the slide. I use a rawhide mallet and give the barrel a sharp rap. When you take it out, you can easily see where it is hitting the slide. Remove only that mark and try again. You will need to remove only a little metal, so go slowly. The goal is for the barrel to go into and out of the battery with no force. I always stop with the hood just a little tight and touch up as needed after test-firing.

As I went along, each barrel setup was test-fired for function with ammunition representative of what would be used in the accuracy-test portion. You may notice that Federal match wadcutter is one of those loads. Conventional wisdom says plain guns won't feed that, and you need a special lighter spring. That is bogus BS. With each barrel, the gun ran perfectly with it using the standard spring. As a concession to convenience, I did replace the standard Springfield two-piece full-length recoil spring guide with a standard guide and plug. When the actual testing is done, I like to leave the frame in the Ransom Rest and simply change barrels, and that facilitates changing—plus I am not a fan of full-length guide rods.

So here was the process I used. When the stock pistol arrived, it was test-fired with all the ammo likely to be used, and it functioned without a hitch. Then the Nowlin Pre-fit barrel was installed, and the test was repeated—again there were no stoppages. Finally, the Kart barrel was fitted and tested in the same manner as the other two. This time I carefully checked for wear or high spots on the barrel, and I took a tiny cut on the hood to make it drop freely. Since there had been an "alteration," the test was repeated. During all of this shooting, there were still no malfunctions.

The test procedure is routine for me and begins with a minimum of 15 rounds to settle the gun in the rest. This period is also used to

As it comes from the supplier, the Kart bushing will not go into the slide. The author uses a belt sander to carefully remove a little metal from the outside diameter of the bushing.

.45 ACP Springfield Loaded 1911A1 Accuracy Results

Factory Load	Velocity (fps)	Extreme Spread (fps)	25-Yard Accuracy (Inches)					Average
			Group 1	Group 2	Group 3	Group 4	Group 5	
Factory Barrel								
Federal 185-gr. Match	780	75	2.09	1.86	1.51	1.13	1.90	1.70
Black Hills 200-gr. LSWC	860	42	2.06	1.94	2.03	2.21	1.98	2.04
Remington UMC 230-gr. FMJ	836	47	4.77	4.07	1.03	2.84	4.16	3.77
Overall Average								2.51
Nowlin Pre-Fit Match Barrel								
Federal 185-gr. Match	786	63	1.43	2.17	1.78	2.40	2.34	1.84
Black Hills 200-gr. LSWC	867	39	2.43	1.99	2.07	2.05	1.90	2.09
Remington UMC 230-gr. FMJ	810	49	1.70	1.62	3.23	2.54	3.07	2.43
Overall Average								2.12
Kart Easy Fit Barrel								
Federal 185-gr. Match	835	49	2.21	1.07	1.24	0.71	1.25	1.30
Black Hills 200-gr. LSWC	876	35	1.90	2.07	1.54	1.27	1.19	1.59
Remington UMC 230-gr. FMJ	829	41	1.24	1.53	1.84	2.08	1.99	1.74
Overall Average								1.54

NOTES: Accuracy data are for five consecutive five-shot groups fired at 25 yards with the pistol mounted in a Ransom Rest. Velocity is the average of 25 rounds measured 15 feet from the gun's muzzle.

verify the proper operation of the chronograph. Normally I chronograph each round but just report the statistics on the entire string—in this case, 25 rounds. And since one of the test loads has a lead bullet, I shoot those last and fire an extra five rounds that are not measured to be sure the bore is conditioned for the ammo change. Even though I am changing only the barrels—not taking the gun out of the rest—I still fire the settling rounds before record shooting begins. In addition, the barrel is lubricated before any shooting, and the procedure is strictly followed for the third barrel as well. This routine produces a lot of information.

Sometimes when you have this much information, it is a challenge just to figure out what it's telling you. The first thing is that you will

see some rather large or small groups within any given set. This falls under the law of random distribution (the bell curve), and if we didn't have that, the data would be suspect. The information really doesn't tell us anything about the quality of the barrel itself but rather how well it fits the gun. The secret to accuracy in the 1911 pistol is in the lockup and the need for the barrel to return to the same place after every shot. The only way to judge the quality of the rifling itself is to test it independent of the gun in a special fixture.

But maybe the biggest question is one the shooter must ask himself. "Do I need to do anything at all to the gun to meet my needs?"

Not too long ago, brand-new guns often shot 5-inch groups at 25 yards and wouldn't have a prayer of working with target loads. Today,

reliable function is a given, and as it came from the box, the Springfield was more than accurate enough for defense or general recreational shooting.

Shooters always want to personalize their guns, but today, there isn't much left to do, and frequently, modification is an expense that produces no tangible benefit. A barrel upgrade is an exception, and better accuracy is the result. I'm especially partial towards the Kart barrel just because it required a little work on my part. The skill required to do this job isn't great, and you can get by nicely with a good file and the installation kit from Kart. If you don't have any experience with a file, find a piece of scrap metal and practice filing a flat surface so you won't end up with the hood all cattywampus.

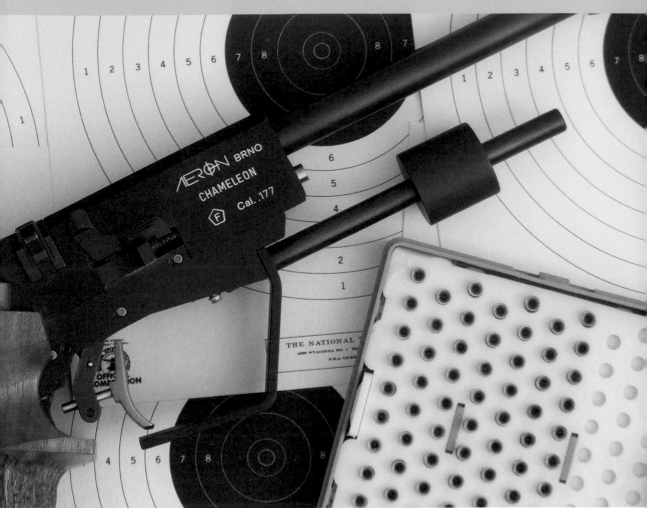

Shooting Airguns Can Improve Your Accuracy

By Tom Gaylord

Let airguns improve your shooting skills—build a safe range in your home.

Simple and easy, that's my motto—but when you shoot firearms, simple isn't always possible. Besides the time spent reloading and associated chores, there is the mountain of logistics involved in going to the range. So much stuff to pack, then load into the car, unload at the range, and carry to the line. And, when you finish shooting, you have to reverse the whole process.

Then there are the mandatory cleaning sessions afterward. I have some rifles that can take time over a two-day period before they are ready to go back on the wall. I therefore find myself weighing the fun I think I'll have against the trouble it takes to make it all happen and, more often than not, I skip the whole deal.

Fortunately, there is an easier alternative. Down in the cool of my basement, I have created a 10-meter airgun range. A variety of action targets await me, though traditional paper bullseyes are by far the target of choice. There are no critics in my basement to comment on my shaky shooting style or lack of fancy equipment. In fact, I have been known to actually stand on my hind legs and shoot at the target like a man on rare occasions.

If you are a shooter, you really should investigate the possibilities of shooting at home as a means of improving your accuracy by honing your shooting skills. Airguns make it possible for just about anybody—even those who don't have basements or large houses.

You may live in an efficiency apartment with the longest straight distance measuring just eight feet—you can still shoot safely and quietly. You just need to adapt your shooting to whatever situation you face. Let me show you how easy it is.

Shooting on a home airgun range in your basement will improve your shooting skills.

Shooting in Big Spaces

For shooters blessed with big basements, long hallways, large garages, attics, and, best of all, large backyards, shooting airguns is a snap. There are the normal safety fundamentals to observe, but within those guidelines, you can improve your shooting skills if you have the room.

One of the nicest things about airguns is that they replicate in a very short space what firearms do over much greater distance. For example, the sport of Olympic free pistol is shot with a .22 rimfire pistol at 50 meters. But target air pistol, which requires equal precision, is shot at 10 meters.

Target air pistols cost about half what free pistols cost, and their ammunition is cheaper by an order of magnitude. The noise and safety distances are equally diminished for the airgunner.

But what about the long-range target shooter? How does a buffalo runner or a varmint shooter equate airguns to his interests? The answer is both surprising and wonderful. You see, a .22-caliber air rifle shooting a 15-grain pellet at 50 yards acts very much like a .45-70 rifle shooting a 405-grain lead bullet at 500 meters.

The time of the pellet's flight is very pronounced; the high arc of the pellet's trajectory mimics the blackpowder bullet, and the drift caused by wind is equally great. The difference is in the scale of the measurements downrange. The .45-70 arcs many feet enroute to the target; the pellet arcs many inches. Wind drift of several feet for the bullet becomes several inches for the pellet. Paper targets that measure many feet in both dimensions can be much smaller for the airgunner, yet they look the same. You can even apply this logic for high-velocity smallbore centerfire cartridges, though they shoot flatter than blackpowder cartridges.

The smaller airgun scale helps in other ways, too. Where a single life-sized steel 500-meter ram silhouette is a heavy load for a man, an airgunner can carry five metal rams conveniently in a shirt pocket. Yet the proportions of scale seem similar for both guns. Only the speed of sound returns the airgun's satisfying clink from 45 yards sooner than the .45-70's clang from 500 meters.

Everything else in this report applies to indoor shooting, but anyone lucky enough to have some safe space outdoors is especially fortunate. And tops on the outdoors list of good places to shoot seems to be the second-story back deck. From it, a shooter can safely shoot all shots into the ground, which is a near-perfect backstop.

I know many shooters who have built up plinking ranges off their back decks with various novelty targets placed around the yard. The most extravagant range I know of is owned by a couple living on a remote island in British Columbia. They have life-sized tree targets placed up to 125 yards from their back deck, yet they are all on a downward angle because of the slope of the land. What luck!

But even if you don't have a deck, a large yard can provide endless airgun shooting possibilities. Another shooter I know has targets hung in a tree at 100 yards from his shooting bench. For him, the shots do not go into the ground, but rather travel to their maximum range over water. It is easy for him to ascertain whether the downrange area is clear and since even the most powerful pellet rifles can only throw their diabolo (wasp-waisted) pellets about 500 yards, there is a positive safe range limit with no danger of ricochet because the pellets are falling to ground (water) at less than 100 fps. Again, this is an unusual circumstance, but a shooter definitely should take advantage of it.

The Bullet Trap of Choice

If you have the space, set up a long airgun range. Buy a .22-rimfire bullet trap similar to the one made by Champion (formerly Outers). This trap will stop a 40-grain lead bullet generating 140 foot-pounds at the muzzle, so it is large enough to safely trap a 32-grain pellet generating 80 foot-pounds. While it will not han-

dle big-bore airguns, anything in .25 caliber and smaller will work fine.

Behind the trap, place a 3/4-inch plywood backer board to absorb any stray shots. I like to use a backer board three feet square at 10 meters, but size yours according to the distance of the bullet trap. Set the board on an angle so the pellet has more than 3/4 inch of wood to penetrate—should it hit.

With a powerful rifle like the Air-Force Talon SS, the board will not completely stop even one pellet (if the gun is shot at high power) but it will slow it down enough to keep it from going through the wall behind it or cracking a cinder block.

I have shot more than half a million times at my Champion trap, and it is just as sound as the day it was made. There are other traps on the market made just for airguns, but many of them are made expressly

for low-power target guns. If you shoot at them with a powerful air rifle, you can destroy them in a very short time.

Shooting in Small Spaces

Before you start worrying about what little space you have, you should know that during World War II, a German submarine was captured and in the captain's cabin they found a Haenel air pistol! Ever been in a World War II-vintage submarine? They make compact cars seem expansive. Unless you live in a doghouse, there should be room to shoot somewhere.

Pick the right airgun and pellet trap and you don't have to worry about sound, either. I used to shoot a target air pistol in an empty classroom adjacent to a classroom full of adults. This was in the mid-1980s, and the building was a commercial

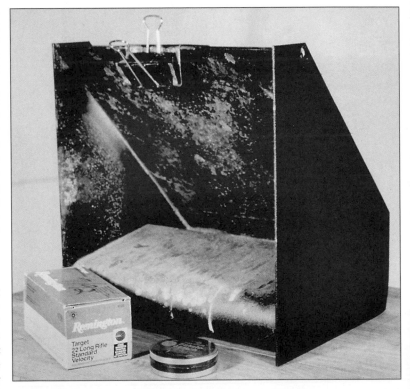

The Champion bullet trap is built to stop a bullet from a .22 rimfire, so it is more than adequate for magnum air rifles in the smaller calibers (.177 through .25).

office building in Baltimore. I shot into a silent pellet trap, and no one ever knew I was there. I shot that same pistol in my private office, which was all of 10x8 feet, with walls made of the finest ticky-tacky, and still no one noticed the noise.

What is a silent trap? It is a container of a dense material called ballistic putty that stops a lead pellet in a very short distance with no sound. A powerful 1000 fps gun will penetrate about an inch into the material while a pussycat will not even bury the pellet completely. Because the material is also very sticky, this is the one trap that will also work for BBs.

The Talon SS from AirForce Airguns is an American-made sporter with interchangeable barrels and adjustable power. It has been used by the U.S. Army Sniper School at Ft. Benning for informal sniper training.

You can make a silent trap easily by making a wooden box from 1x3 lumber. Fasten a steel plate cut from a cookie sheet on the back of the target and add a half inch plywood sheet over that. The interior dimensions should be 6 inches wide and 9 inches tall for a nice trap. Fill the trap with 6 pounds of duct seal, which you can find at electrical contractor supply houses.

The goal is to have an even sheet of material about 1.5 to 2 inches deep. That will safely stop pellets from guns as powerful as 15 foot-pounds, which is a .177 rifle shooting an 8-grain pellet at about 920 fps. Most so-called "1000 fps" guns will be hard-pressed to achieve this velocity.

From time to time, clean the trap by removing the pellets that have fused together into large lumps of

The silent pellet trap is just a box filled with duct seal. The opening of this one measures 6 inches across and 9 inches high. Note the well-used backer board here.

lead. As the hits start building in the duct seal material, it will soon be impossible to remove them all when you clean the trap, and those that remain will only strengthen the trap. I have a silent trap made exactly as described here that can now stop a 30 foot-pound air rifle with ease.

If you don't want to build a silent trap, they are available over the counter from many of the better-stocked airgun suppliers, such as Pyramid Air Inc.

Targets

There are also a wide variety of other traps and novelty targets for the home shooter. In fact, some specialized traps incorporate the novelty targets in a single package!

Every American airgun manufacturer and Gamo has a full line of home traps and novelty targets for their airguns. Check online catalogs of Beeman, Crosman, Daisy, Marksman, and Gamo to see what's available.

For the absolute in precision, shoot at 10-meter air rifle or air pistol paper targets. These are the same targets that world-cup shooters engage; and if you have the whole 10-meter distance to shoot, the only difference will be your scores.

The 10-meter rifle target has a bull considerably smaller than the NRA 50-foot Small Bore target, and the scoring rings are considerably smaller. The 10-ring is a dot that's smaller than the period at the end of this sentence. It's so small, in fact,

that shooters fire only one pellet at each bull to keep the scoring uncomplicated. Yet the competition is so intense that the typical score for 60 shots by world-class shooters hovers around 591.

Ten-meter pistol targets have bulls somewhat smaller than the NRA 50-foot Timed Fire pistol target, and the 10-ring is about the size of a pencil eraser. It's quite challenging when you hold the pistol in one hand, which the rules require. Still, at the world-class level, a score of 580 for 60 shots will guarantee close to last place.

Airgun competition is so keen at the World Cup and Olympics that paper targets are no longer scored by hand. The target holders have three sound transducers that sense the tearing of the target paper when the pellet passes through. They then triangulate the location of the pellet strike to the thousandth of an inch and relay that to both the shooter's monitor and to the match officials. The shooter sees a target on screen with a representation of each hit.

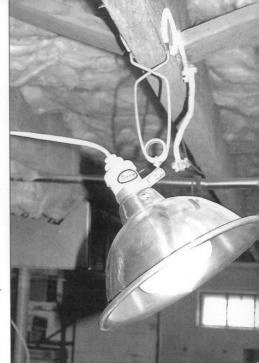

Lighting is important on a home airgun range, but it doesn't need to be expensive. Clip-on light fixtures with 75-watt floodlight bulbs work very well.

An international 10-meter air rifle target has small scoring rings yet top shooters miss the 10-ring (dot at the center) less than 10 times in 60 shots.

The 10-ring of an air pistol target is about the size of a .177-caliber pellet. Try hitting that every time from 33 feet!

Lighting

Lighting is important on a home range, but it doesn't need to be fancy or expensive. You will shoot best if the target is well lit. General room lighting is seldom good for this, so visit the hardware store and buy a cheap clip-on fixture

with an aluminum bowl reflector. A single light bulb works well in these, but a floodlight works even better. Mine is 75 watts and I have it clipped to a joist about 6 feet from the target.

At the shooting line, you need enough light to see what you are doing but not so much that it disturbs your sighting or puts a flare on the objective lens of your scope. The darker it is at the shooter's station, the more vivid the sights and target will be.

Safety

The safety considerations on a home range are the same as for any range, plus a few unique ones. First and foremost, be sure of what you are shooting at. Never guess that your pellet won't penetrate a backer board because I have seen several situations where concrete walls were peppered with pellet divots before the shooter even knew what was happening.

If you shoot from a benchrest, the trap looks too large to miss at 10 meters, but I have missed mine several times. Do not make a mistake here. The home range requires a generous spirit on the part of all inhabitants of the house, and you want to preserve their trust at all costs.

Be sensitive to the possibility for ricochets on your range. The best bullet trap in the world is of no help if you shoot at metal targets inside it.

> "If you decide to build an airgun range in your home, proceed slowly and always keep safety foremost in your mind. Once you begin to use the range, though, you'll wonder why you haven't been shooting at home all along."

If you want to shoot at metal targets in the house, get one of the specialty traps engineered for it and use airguns of an appropriately low power level.

When a lead projectile hits a hard backstop at greater than 700 fps, it shatters into tiny fragments. At higher speeds, some of the lead particles will flash when they are heated to the point of incandescence. This will look like sparks to the shooter.

The point is that the floor and area surrounding the bullet trap will soon be covered by lead dust from the shattering of many pellets. Be considerate and clean up the mess before a pet or family member tracks it into another part of your house.

Is your range engineered so an unsuspecting adult will not be able to suddenly walk in front of the pellet trap without warning? Maybe you and your wife are familiar with range operations, but what if a couple of visitors are shooting and your brother-in-law suddenly walks into the room? Will he be in danger?

What about your children? I'm sure you are smart enough to keep your kids away from the trap during a shooting session, but what happens when the toddler is playing on the floor while your wife does the laundry? Are there lead fragments to ingest? Can the steel pellet trap be grabbed as a handhold for Junior to steady himself in preparation for a walk?

And, what about your pets? You probably have the fish under control, but what about the bird and the cat? We once had a female cat with sensitive ears who objected to the noise made by my louder airguns.

Her method of communication was to suddenly jump into the bullet trap while I was shooting! She was so stealthy that I seldom saw her approach, so I had to always be on guard. Later, she learned to jump on my shooting bench and stare directly at me. That was better from a safety standpoint, but still unnerving.

Consider sound safety on your home range. The air rifle that sounds so quiet outdoors will reverberate off the walls of your basement and surprise you. I have been known to wear hearing protection on my range when shooting a particularly loud airgun. Candidate guns are most CO2-powered guns, most pneumatics and some powerful rifles equipped with gas springs.

Noise suppression isn't just for safety on the home range, either. It's also a courtesy to other family members to keep from disturbing them with your shooting. In fact, the strongest objection to having a shooting range in the house, after safety, is the noise.

When I test a particularly loud airgun on my range, I wait until I am alone in the house, then herd all the animals upstairs and close the door. Since this activity creates an intense curiosity among our cats, I finish my shooting quickly and open the door again for a full inspection of the premises. Believe me—I get one!

Hopefully, you have been convinced that a home airgun range is a safe and desirable thing. If you decide to build one in your home, proceed slowly and always keep safety foremost in your mind. Once you begin to use the range, though, you'll wonder why you haven't been shooting at home all along.

10 Easy Steps To Muzzleloader Accuracy & Reliability

By Layne Simpson

Following these steps should help you enjoy maximum accuracy from your muzzleloader.

They say hard lessons learned when we are young are the ones we remember longest. One lesson I learned at an earlier age (and will never forget) is the importance of properly maintaining a muzzleloader. Back when the Thompson/Center Hawken had been on the market for only a few years, I subjected one to rather extensive accuracy tests a few days prior to opening day of deer season. Then giving it nothing more than a lick and a promise rather than a thorough cleaning, I took that rifle deer hunting. As you have probably already guessed, my laziness cost me a very nice buck when the rifle misfired on opening morning.

What you are about to read are several reasons why that has not happened to me again while hunting with a percussion rifle. Some of the tips also may help you to enjoy maximum accuracy from your rifle.

Clean the Bore

1 A deep bucket filled with hot water and a bit of dishwashing detergent is still the best way to clean the barrel of a muzzleloader—especially if the barrel is easily removed from the stock. If not, various cleaners

Keeping your muzzleloader's bore clean is important for good accuracy. Bore cleaners like those from Remington and Hodgdon do a good job of cleaning out powder fouling, and Layne has found that Shooter's Choice's Shotgun Cleaner works well for removing residue from plastic sabots.

designed for just that purpose are more convenient. Hodgdon's EZ Clean, which is formulated to dissolve fouling left behind by Pyrodex, is excellent. So is Vortex from Remington.

Water-based cleaners such as those available from Hodgdon and Remington do a good job of dissolving powder fouling, but none I am aware of were designed to remove the plastic fouling left behind by plastic sabots. Some sabots are made of extremely soft material. When they are pushed to "three-Pyrodex-Pellet" speeds, as many who hunt with .50-caliber in-line rifles are doing, they leave heavy, accuracy-destroying deposits clinging stubbornly to the bore. And it takes only a few rounds to do the damage. Any bore cleaner designed to dissolve or lift plastic works here, and one of the best I have used is Shotgun and Choke Tube Cleaner from Shooter's Choice. Just spray it down the bore, allow it to work for a minute, and then brush the bore vigorously. A paste called J B Non-Embedding Bore Cleaning Compound from Brownells also works quite well. Simply coat a cotton patch with it and whisk the plastic buildup from the bore with a cleaning rod.

Protect the Scope

2 I actually prefer to hunt with the old-time percussion rifles, and my favorites are Thompson/Center creations. One is a Hawken in .50 caliber. It is still available. The others are the wonderfully lightweight little Cherokee and Seneca, both in .45 caliber and both discontinued long ago. This is unfortunate because I consider them to be the '94 Winchesters of traditional-styled muzzleloaders.

I learned the hard way that when I hunt with a modern in-line muzzleloader wearing a scope, the finish of the scope can take a real beating as it gets blasted by smoke and particles escaping through the nipple. Some rifles are worse than others in this respect. If your rifle is prone to this, wrapping a couple of layers of plastic electrical tape around the tube of the scope is one solution. The tape won't be pretty, but it will protect the finish of the scope.

Keep The Bore Rust-Free Without Misfires

Some of the old-fashioned gun oils did a great job of preventing metal from rusting, but when applied to the bore of a muzzleloader barrel, they could contaminate the powder charge to the point that only partial ignition would occur. If enough was slopped into the bore, the powder might not ignite at all.

Products I have used with complete satisfaction are Remington's Rem Oil, Rust Guard from Midway, Sheath by Birchwood Casey, Rust Prevent from Shooter's Choice, Tetra Gun lubricant from FTI, Corrosion X from Corrosion Technologies, and Outers Gunslick Tri-Lube.

A seized breechplug makes cleaning from the breech end difficult. The threads of the breechplug should be cleaned of powder fouling and coated with an antiseize agent each time it is removed from the gun's receiver.

Those are applied to the bore with a cotton patch and cleaning rod after the bore has been properly cleaned. Heating the barrel with a hair dryer prior to applying the rust preventative seems to cause it to soak in even better. Since most modern rust-preventative products actually penetrate the pores of steel, it is not necessary to leave a heavy coat on the surface of the metal to prevent rust. After the barrel cools down, I thoroughly dry out its bore with several clean, dry patches. And because the rust inhibitor is in the metal rather than on it, there is little to no possibility that it will affect the performance of the powder charge.

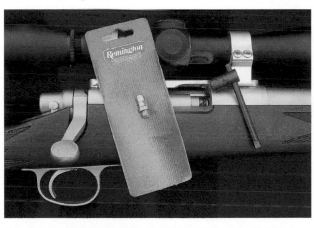

Because the nipple gets peened and pounded by repeated firing, Layne recommends using one nipple for practice shooting and then replacing it with a new one for hunting.

Keep the Bore Rust-Free without Misfires

3 I have found that a very thin film of some of today's rust inhibitors left in the bore will have no detrimental effect on either blackpowder or Pyrodex.

Hunt with a New Nipple

4 After the nipple of a muzzleloader has been pounded by the hammer numerous times, it can get peened and bat-

tered to the point where its orifice is partially plugged. If the nipple also becomes shortened from repeated poundings, the cap may not receive the full blow of the hammer. This is why it is best to install a new nipple in your rifle when hunting with it. I always test a new nipple during a practice session to make sure everything is in order, and then I clean it thoroughly. From that point on, it is reserved for nothing but hunting.

Keep the Breechplug from Seizing

5 The breechplugs of some in-line muzzleloaders are easily removed. This is a great feature because it allows me to clean rifles such as the Remington

A common problem with well-used muzzleloaders is rifling wear at the muzzle due to cleaning the bore from the muzzle end. If you must clean your gun from the muzzle, be sure to use a cleaning rod bore guide.

Model 700 ML and Savage Model 10ML from the breech end, thereby avoiding possible cleaning rod wear on the rifling at the muzzle. Each time a breechplug is removed, its threads and the threads in the barrel should be thoroughly cleaned of powder fouling. Then, unless you want the plug to stay in forever, its threads should be coated with some type of antiseize product before it is screwed back into the barrel. Thompson/Center offers several of

those antiseize products. One comes in a squeeze tube and is called All Purpose Anti-Seize Super Lube. My favorite is Gorilla Grease, not because it is better than the other one, but because it smells good and I like its name. Thin Teflon tape wrapped around the threads of the breechplug will also keep if from seizing. Also available from T/C, it is called EZ-Thread Anti-Seize Tape. Special lubes designed to prevent a screw-in choke from seizing in a shotgun barrel also work quite well here.

Use a Breech Thread Protector When Cleaning

6 When cleaning the barrel of an in-line muzzleloader from its breech end—as should always be done, if possible—the breechplug threads in the barrel are subject to wear from the cleaning rod. Pulling dirty patches across those threads can also fill them with difficult-to-remove gunk. To prevent any of this from happening, you should always turn a special cleaning rod guide into the breech threads before starting your cleaning program. My Remington Model 700ML came with such a breech thread protector, but for rifles made by manufacturers who are not so considerate, Thompson/Center offers a plastic version that fits a number of different rifles.

Avoid Rifling Wear at the Muzzle

7 Few hunters will ever shoot a muzzleloader enough to burn out its barrel, but I'd say many barrels are worn out by ramrods and cleaning rods every year. To avoid unnecessary wear on that critical part of the rifling at the muzzle, always use a brass rod guide when loading the rifle during practice sessions and when cleaning its barrel. Several companies offer such a gizmo. (The only time you would not want to use a rod guide when loading a rifle from the muzzle is when you miss buck, boar, or bear with the first shot and are reloading as quickly as possible.)

Use the Hottest Ignition System Available

8 An entire article could be written on the pros and cons of the various types of nipples, caps, and primers now being used by hunters. For now, I will simply say that any hunter who uses Pyrodex should also use the hottest priming system available for that rifle. In some cases this may mean replacing the nipple that was installed in the rifle at the factory. In other cases it might mean switching to another type of cap or primer. Playing around with mild ignition systems for paper target shooting is one thing, but only the hotter systems offer the reliability needed

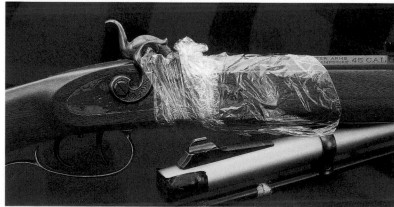

Plastic sandwich wrap over the capped nipple and plastic electrical tape over the muzzle do a fine job of protecting the powder charge from dampness and keeping your muzzleloader shooting when the rains come.

when using Pyrodex in all types of weather conditions.

Weatherproof Your Rifle

9 I have hunted with percussion rifles in downpours that would cause a fish to cling to a life preserver, but I have yet to experience a misfire. The secret is to seal off the bore of the rifle and its nipple from the elements. For that job I haven't found anything better than plastic electrical tape and cling-type plastic food wrap. Food wrap goes by several different names, but the most common brands in my neck of the woods are Saran Wrap and Stretch-Tite.

Here is how to keep your rifle shooting when the rains come. I seal off the muzzle end of the bore by wrapping a strip of the plastic electrical tape over the outside of the muzzle. To make sure the plastic tape holds its watertight seal and stays in place in the field, I wrap it tightly with a rubber band. This type of muzzle cover does not have to be removed prior to firing as air pushed

> **"To avoid unnecessary wear on that critical part of the rifling at the muzzle, always use a brass rod guide when loading the rifle during practice sessions and when cleaning its barrel."**

ahead of the ball or bullet will blast away the tape before the projectile gets to the muzzle. At the rear, I use a couple layers of plastic food wrap to keep the capped nipple high and dry. A couple of rubber bands, one behind the nipple and the other in front of it, keep the wrap in place and help to keep water out. Don't worry about removing the plastic before shooting as it will not cushion the blow of the hammer on the cap enough to cause a misfire.

Hunt with a Fresh Charge

10 Even when using those weatherproofing procedures, hunting in rainy weather for days on end with the same powder charge in my rifle makes me nervous. If the weather is really bad and the rifle and I get really wet, I will pull the bullet at the end of the day, dump the powder charge, and discard the percussion cap or primer. I will then clean the rifle inside and out. Before loading it I will allow it to thoroughly dry out while sitting close to the fire in my tent or cabin. Come morning, I start another day of hunting with a fresh powder charge and cap or primer.

When hunting in areas of extremely high humidity (like in the Deep South), I seldom leave a powder charge in my rifle for more than three days even when it does not rain. All of this is probably unnecessary in most cases, but the way I see it, if starting fresh each day prevents just one misfire during a lifetime of hunting, the procedure is worthwhile.

So now you know why I have not experienced a misfire with a muzzleloading rifle in many years. I hope these tips and techniques will help you be just as lucky.

ACCURACY FACT: MATCH-GRADE BULLETS VERSUS HUNTING-GRADE BULLETS

BY LAYNE SIMPSON

When it comes to accuracy, a lot of what we often think is true will never be carved into granite simply because too many uncontrollable variables are involved, but I'd like to share some of the most common accuracy facts and fallacies that readers have written to me about over the years. An important one is match-grade bullets versus hunting-grade bullets.

The major bulletmakers offer match-grade bullets in certain calibers. Based on their classification alone, one might logically assume them to be more accurate in all rifles than hunting-grade bullets. Theoretically speaking, this is true, but in actual practice hunting rifles are as accurate, and sometimes even more so, with standard bullets.

Many good hunting-grade bullets, particularly those in calibers ranging from .224 to .308, are inherently capable of less than 1/2-minute-of-angle (MOA) accuracy

while some match bullets will consistently land in groups smaller than a quarter-inch. The difference might be considered great by a long-range target shooter because a quarter-inch deviation at 100 yards increases to 2.50 inches at 1000. But the difference is insignificant to varmint shooters and big-game hunters who are concerned with shots at much closer ranges. On top of that, it takes a level of accuracy unobtainable with most factory rifles to tell any difference between the two types of bullets.

Even when both bullets are fired in extremely accurate target rifles, the difference is often virtually impossible to detect out to 500 yards. The accuracy limitations of hunting-weight rifles can and often does vary enough to wash out the slight accuracy edge of match bullets. These limitations, combined with individual rifle preferences, often causes hunting rifles to shoot considerably smaller groups with hunting bullets than with the match variety.

Groove Your Move

By Greg Rodriguez

These proven tips will improve your sporting clays scores.

Mastering the gun mount and the move to the target will improve your wingshooting skills.

Though I make my living with a rifle, walking behind well-trained pointers with a lithe, sexy scattergun is one of my greatest pleasures. Unfortunately, I don't get to do it as much as I'd like because my television and magazine commitments keep me busy hunting big game or guiding hunters 180 to 200 days each year. I am still as passionate about hunting four-legged critters as I was when I took my first buck 27 years ago, but I often find myself counting the days until my next dove or quail hunt.

Because I only get to shoot birds a few times each year, I try to sneak off to shoot skeet or sporting clays whenever I can. I wasn't the greatest wing shot when I started shooting sporting clays, but I improved rapidly once I started shooting regularly. Unfortunately, I hit a wall just as fast and no matter how much I practiced, I couldn't get any better.

My main problem was that I was wildly inconsistent. I would shoot nine or 10 targets on one station and two on the next station or, even worse, hit just one or two on a station I'd smoked nine or 10 on the day before. I learned the hard way that my inconsistency was largely related to bad habits and poor training.

One of my big issues was cross-dominance. I was born left-handed, but learned to do everything with my right. When it comes to my hands, I am pretty much ambidextrous. My eyes, however, are not. My strong left-eye dominance, combined with starting with my gun pointing at the trap so I was always behind every bird, made all the targets seem fast as lightning and made it tough to focus. I tried to shoot my way through my problems, but all that shooting just served to frustrate me even more.

I asked some experienced shooters I know for their advice. A few well-intentioned but misguided souls offered shooting tips, but the smart ones recommended that I seek quality instruction. A few also suggested I get a gun that fit me properly. I am short and stocky, and I'd noticed that my old gun hung up on my shoulder from time to time, so I decided to get a new one and have it fitted before I spent lots of time and money on instruction.

Gun Fit Makes A Difference

I shot a semiauto for skeet and sporting clays for many years. I still like that gun, but I almost always hunt with a double, so I decided I should be shooting clays with one, too. After trying one out at a charity clays shoot and talking with several well-known competitors about it, I decided Blaser's F3 was the perfect gun for me.

The F3 is a beautiful gun with a great stock design that seems to fit me well, a fantastic trigger, and a low-profile receiver that looks good and fits perfectly in my small hands. The ability to order one with gorgeous wood and extra barrel sets that have the same weight and balance as the 30-inch, 12-gauge tubes I shoot clays with also appealed to me.

I ordered my Blaser from Alamo Sporting Arms in San Antonio, which is quite close to the offices of Blaser USA. When the gun came in, I picked it up and drove over to Blaser to get fitted by Rich Kaysa, Blaser USA's VP of sales and marketing. Kaysa is also a gunsmith and world-class trap shooter. In fact, he won the 100th Grand American Clay Target Championship in 1999, so he knows a thing or two about gun fit.

Kaysa says proper gun fit, regardless of which gun you choose, is essential to success on the range and in the field. The biggest benefits are a smoother mount and a gun that shoots where you look, but a properly fitted gun also minimizes felt recoil. It doesn't matter if you just chop off the stock on your old 870 to a more manageable length or have a fine, custom-fitted double,

Rich Kaysa of Blaser (right) discusses the try-gun Blaser uses to fit shooters. The almost infinitely adjustable stock helps trained stock fitters get a perfect fit. The author likes the Blaser F3 because it has a sleek, trim action and gorgeous wood.

the better your gun fits you, the better you'll shoot.

To fit my gun, Kaysa spent a great deal of time watching me mount my new Blaser, making notes and taking measurements. When he finished, we left the gun and his notes with Blaser's in-house gunsmith while we went to lunch. When we returned, my new gun was waiting for me. A few practice mounts in the shop were all it took for me to see that my F3 fit me perfectly.

That weekend, I shot a few practice rounds with my new Blaser and a friend's F3 that hadn't been shortened or modified in any way. I was considerably smoother and hit more targets with my fitted gun, and the 30-inch barrels helped it swing much more smoothly for me than my old 28-inch semiauto. I was pleased to see that the effort I took to have my gun fitted was justified. I only hoped I could get such noticeable results from my upcoming lessons.

Good Instruction Counts

I didn't have to go far to find top-notch instruction because famed instructors Gil and Vicki Ash of the OSP School (www.ospschool. com) teach at my home range, American Shooting Centers. I've actually known the Ashes for years, and I even took a class from Gil a few years ago. I really like their commonsense approach and their in-depth understanding of how the eye, mind, and body work together, so choosing them was a no-brainer.

I couldn't possibly convey all the things I learned over the two months I trained with the Ashes in this article even if I was qualified to teach it (I'm not). But I would like to pass along a few of the things they taught me that led to major improvements in my shooting.

Two Important Skills

Two of the things the Ashes stress above all others are (1) a good gun mount and (2) your move to the target. It all starts with the gun at the ready and the muzzle just under the target's line of flight. The barrel should start out pointing well in front of the trap, and your eyes should be focused just in front of the machine so you can pick up the target as soon as it comes out of the trap. When you see the bird, smoothly swing your gun towards the break point while bringing the gun to your shoulder and focusing hard on the front edge of the clay. Your muzzle should stay out front and your swing should be fluid and in time with the target while mounting the gun. Do not mount then swing or swing then mount and then swing some more—it must all be done simultaneously.

I cannot stress enough how important it is to keep your muz-

Vicki Ash has her eyes on the target while matching its speed with her shotgun. Note that the gun has just hit her shoulder as her eyes follow the bird.

zle in front of and on line with the target. The swing-through style, which has you starting behind the bird, swinging past it and squeezing the trigger is, perhaps, the leading cause of inconsistency because it is so darn tough to repeat. That's why swing-through shooters tend to be so streaky. Keeping your muzzle in front of and on the same level as the target is much easier to repeat than the swing-through method and leads to more consistent results.

Gil is adamant about the importance of picking a break point before you ever call for the bird and squeezing the trigger when the target reaches it. The break point serves as a reference point that makes it easier for your eye and mind to work together. Selecting a break point made a big difference in my hit rates. In fact, I've broken more birds with a bad mount at the break point than I have with a perfect mount on birds I swung with too long. Shooting a shotgun is instinctive, so taking too long to fire can sometimes allow your mind to ruin a perfectly good gun mount. Learn to trust your mount—when the gun hits your shoulder and the bird is at the break point, smash it.

Starting with your gun near the break point reduces the amount of gun movement required to break the target. Since I started shooting that way, my gun moves very little and I feel much smoother and in control. In fact, several of my friends have commented on my new-found smoothness and how little my gun moves.

Gil constantly preaches the importance of laser-like target focus. "If you see the gun, you'll miss" is his mantra. Focusing hard on the bird while moving in time with it allows your eye, mind, and body to work together to automatically calculate the lead and make the shot. If you see the bead of your gun, your focus isn't sharp enough and you will miss. That little nugget was pure gold for this cross-dominant shooter because it takes eye dominance out of play. If you focus on the bird and trust your move, you'll break the bird no matter which eye has the sharper focus.

Another benefit of staying in front of the bird and having a hard focus on the target is that the birds appear to move very slowly. Those two little tricks have eliminated the

Peripheral Acceptance • Break Point

Correct

This is a great illustration of how little gun movement it takes to break birds if you start with your gun close to the break point. The clay marked "1" is about where your eyes should be when you call for the bird. (Illustration courtesy of Gil and Vicki Ash)

Incorrect

10 TIPS FOR BETTER WINGSHOOTING

1. Bring the gun to your face, not the other way around.
2. Never start from behind a bird—it only makes them look faster.
3. Pick a break point before you ever call for the bird.
4. Shotgunning should be instinctive, so quit thinking and squeeze the trigger when the gun is comfortably on your shoulder.
5. Focus. Hard. Stare so hard you can see the bird's eye or the ridges on the front of the target.
6. A fitted gun shoots where you look.
7. Your mount will be smoother and you'll get to the target faster if you grip the gun loosely.
8. If you see the gun, you'll miss. Focus on the target.
9. Target speed – barrel speed.
10. Conscious follow-through creates excessive gun speed. Let your gun stop naturally.

desperate feeling I used to get when I started with my gun pointed at the machine and those hard crossers came whizzing by at what seemed like 200 miles per hour.

Follow-through is often discussed and rarely understood. According to Ash, it is simply "the momentum the gun has as the trigger is pulled." Gil says being conscious of follow-through creates excessive gun speed and leads to misses. Don't stop the instant you press the trigger, but don't swing unnaturally long either. Instead, let the gun stop when it wants.

The Proof

Training with the Ashes hasn't made a huge difference in my scoring average, but I wasn't too bad to begin with. I have upped my average by five or six birds a round, but the main improvement in my game is consistency. Thanks to Gil and my new Blaser F3, I don't shoot ones or twos much these days.

Another change is that there are no birds on the course I can't break. Last fall, I shot with Gil on a very challenging course where they'd shot a major national tournament the previous weekend. I am absolutely sure I wouldn't have come close to some of those tough targets a year before, but with Gil, I was able to break every presentation. I didn't break them every time, but I didn't walk away from a single station with a zero or a one. Some of the highly

regarded shooters who competed in that tournament can't say the same.

Because I have such a hard focus on the targets and stay in front of the bird, I feel absolutely in control at every station. The birds appear so slow now that I no longer feel the sense of urgency or panic that used to eat at my gut on really fast targets. I'm breaking more birds now, and I am breaking them quicker, closer, and with less effort than ever before.

I still have a lot of room for improvement, but I finally feel like I'm on the right track. I don't have hopes of being a serious competitive shooter, but I set out to improve enough to be an asset to my charity

shoot team and avoid embarrassing myself. I'm grateful to Gil Ash and Blaser for helping me achieve my not-so-lofty goals.

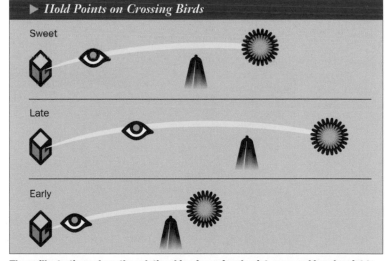

Hold Points on Crossing Birds

Sweet

Late

Early

These illustrations show the relationship of your focal point, gun, and break point to break the target in the sweet spot (top), late (center), or early (bottom). Breaking the bird early requires more lead than you think. (Illustration courtesy of Gil and Vicki Ash)

Get Your Head In The Clouds

Seeing shot patterns from a new angle may help you improve your wingshooting performance.

By Terry Wieland

(Photo courtesy Gil and Vicki Ash)

Understanding shotgun chokes and patterns would be a whole lot easier if we could just see exactly what it is we are talking about.

The problem is, we can't. We can't see a pattern of shot while it is in the air, and even if we could, what we saw one nano-second would be changed significantly a nano-second later and no longer in existence, in any form, a second after that.

This fact, more than any other, has fed the lively arguments over chokes, shot sizes, forcing cones, and myriad other changeable factors in shotgun shooting virtually from the time choke was invented in the 1870s.

Although Americans like to think choke was invented by Fred Kimble in 1868, the idea showed up two years earlier in England, patented by gunmaker William Rochester Pape. We can be charitable and assume that Kimble happened on the idea independently, albeit after Pape.

Today, the notion that patterns can be improved by constricting the muzzle of a shotgun may seem so obvious that it's a wonder it wasn't hatched the day after the first load of shot was fired, but that is true of so many things. The wheel, for example. What could be more obvious? But look how many cultures never invented it at all.

The concept of choke has been refined considerably since Pape's day. Early guns had one barrel marked "Choke," denoting a constriction of about .035 inch, and one barrel left unmarked since the alternative to Choke was nothing at all. It was more or less Cylinder (Cyl.), with a constriction of maybe .002 to .005 inch, but early guns were not marked as such.

In England, gunmakers went on to refine choke to degrees measured in fractions—1/4, 1/2, and 3/4. In America, we developed Improved Cylinder (IC) and Modified (M) as the rough equivalents of 1/4 and

(Top) Gil and Vicki Ash's three-dimensional pattern displays vividly illustrate how effective "killing" choke develops from the muzzle, reaches its peak, and disappears. From left, patterns from Cyl., Skeet, IC, Mod., and Full chokes. The disks are color-coded to indicate distance from the muzzle and carefully sized to the exact diameter of the killing pattern at that distance. Distance in yards: orange, 10; yellow, 15; caramel, 20; red, 25; maroon, 30; medium blue, 35; dark blue, 40; gray, 45; dark gray, 50. (Bottom) Viewed from the rear, it is equally startling to see the way killing patterns drop off.

1/2. Later, Skeet #1 and #2 were developed purely for skeet shooting, and these constrictions lay between Cyl. and IC.

With the advent of interchangeable choke tubes in the 1980s, makers began to refine the divisions farther and farther, splitting hairs and then splitting them again. Eventually, some marked the constrictions in thousandths, with one tube marked .010, another .015, and so on. Other than adding to the confusion, such divisions have little real impact on how well a shotgunner is likely to do on any given day, whether he is shooting sporting clays, doves over a sunflower field, or woodcock in thick cover.

If you center your pattern on your target, it will make no difference whether your choke is Cylinder or Full. None. However, this does not head off the endless arguments over what choke is appropriate for what use, and that brings us back to the problem outlined above: We cannot see exactly what it is we are arguing about, and so we are free to imagine what happens and then propound that point of view.

Shot Pattern Analysis

The traditional method of measuring a shot pattern is to put up a sheet of paper at 40 yards, fire a load of shot at it, then draw a 30-inch circle around the greatest concentration and count the pellet holes. Relative choke is determined by the percentage of pellets inside the circle compared to the number in the original shot charge. An ounce of #7½s contains 345 pellets; if 242 pellets fall within the circle, that is 70 percent, and hence a Full choke.

There are many shortcomings with this method. For one thing, a sheet of paper is a flat surface, and a shot pattern is three-dimensional. Not all the pellets pierce the paper at the same time. You have no idea how long the pattern is. And actually, if time is the fourth dimension, then a shotgun pattern is four-dimensional—changing continuously as time passes.

The usual accepted ideal for a shot pattern is one that is as long as it is wide and tall—more or less shaped like a beach ball flying through the air. Of course, the pattern evolves continuously after it leaves the muzzle, and even if it attains this shape, it will only retain it for a split second. Hence the 40-yard standard: That is where we would generally, more or less, like our ideal pattern to occur, so that is where we measure it.

Still, two patterns, one close to ideal and the other hideously ragged and elongated, could give identical results when measured on a sheet of paper with a 30-inch circle. Obviously, some better method was needed.

Bob Brister, the writer and shotgun authority, tried to determine the shape of a pattern by firing it at a huge surface that was moving sideways, thereby determining the distance between the leading pellet and the last and giving a rough idea of the pattern's overall shape. This was an improvement, but it was difficult, haphazard (affected as it was by both the velocity of the shot and the speed of the target), and very time consuming.

Brister's work did inspire other researchers, however, trying a variety of methods.

Gil and Vicki Ash, two shotgun instructors from Houston, Texas, took up where Brister left off and, about 15 years ago, began a long process of serious shooting, measuring, and counting in order to find out exactly what a shotgun pattern looks like, from the muzzle to beyond normal killing range. They wanted to find out how each pattern evolves and how it is affected by choke.

What the Ashes discovered, they have described in a number of books and videos, as well as applying it on their instruction range near Houston. When I saw Gil's presentation on chokes in August 2009, it struck me as the first really original findings on chokes and patterns that I have seen in the last 20 years.

The Most Useful Choke

After the invention of choke, double guns were marketed for many years with standard configurations. First came Choke & Cyl.; later came IC/M (usually with shorter barrels) or M/F (with longer barrels). In the U.K., 1/4 & 1/2 was common, or 1/2 and Full.

For skeet shooting, even IC was not open enough, and the wide-open Skeet chokes were substituted

IC develops the classic cone-shaped pattern we all imagine, but it is the only choke that does. It reaches its widest killing pattern (maroon) at 30 yards and drops off rapidly thereafter. At 35 yards, its killing pattern is the same size as Modified's, and at 40 yards, Modified choke has a larger killing pattern than IC.

Comparing Modified and Full: Modified develops a killing pattern sooner and holds it longer. No wonder it is such an effective choke for trap shooters.

on serious skeet guns. In trap shooting, where the target is far away and getting farther, Full choke is favored, with some better shooters choosing Extra Full (80 percent) to ensure more concentration of shot and more spectacularly crushed birds.

However—and this is noteworthy—many a trap shooter has posted consistently excellent scores using Modified choke. And not just novices, either. These guys knew instinctively what others did not, but which the Ashes' tests showed definitively: Modified may well be the single most useful choke of all. And here's why.

Most of us imagine the evolving shape of a shot pattern as simply a cloud that starts to spread, either quickly or slowly, as soon as it leaves the muzzle. A few of the more sophisticated imagine it as a spreading cone. In our imaginations, IC gives a wide cone, Full choke a narrow cone.

Not so, say Gil and Vicki Ash. In fact, anything but. First, they determined the concentration of pellets per square inch that denotes a "killing" pattern. Then they traced killing patterns for each choke. They looked at Cyl., Skeet, IC, Mod., and Full chokes, measuring the impact of the pellets at 5-yard increments starting at 10 yards from the muzzle.

The first, and most startling finding, was that every choke maintains a killing concentration of pellets in the center extending straight out from the muzzle—and does so well beyond the usual 40-yard limit. Anyone who has patterned guns knows that the main concentration of shot in any pattern lies in the center—roughly a 15-inch-diameter circle. This concentration of shot, in what is in effect a 15-inch tunnel, is common to all chokes and extends from the muzzle to the end of the pattern's effective life.

Choke does not affect this "core" pattern, only the pellets around the outside. So imagine cones. And now imagine a 15-inch cylinder straight through the middle of each. This rule applies to every choke, from the most open to the most constricted. Choke affects only what happens to the rest of the pellets in the shot load. How those pellets spread, and how quickly, determines the optimum killing pattern and range for each choke. But each choke has a distinct "core" killing pattern and an outer killing pattern.

In the case of Full choke, the pattern expands slowly in a shape that resembles a trumpet. Once the pattern starts to really spread—at around 30 yards—it spreads quickly

and maintains a good killing pattern out to 50 yards.

Cylinder, as might be expected, expands very quickly and gives its greatest killing pattern (30 inches) at 25 yards; by 30 yards, the killing pattern has dropped off to only 20 inches, and beyond 30 yards you have only the "core" of about 15 inches. Skeet choke resembles Cyl. very closely but still has a 16-inch killing pattern at 35 yards.

Improved Cylinder is the only choke tested that delivers the classic, perfect cone—expanding into a noticeable pattern at 10 yards and spreading uniformly out to 30 yards where it delivers a 30-inch killing pattern. By 35 yards, however, the pattern has dropped off to only 20 inches.

The real surprise, to me at least and, I believe, to most other shotgunners, is the performance of Modified. The pattern spreads steadily from the muzzle until, at 25 yards, it is a good 25-inch killing pattern. It then maintains this outer killing pattern for a full 20 yards, neither spreading further nor deteriorating, and giving excellent performance from 25 yards to 45 yards, and a still-creditable 20 inches way out there at 50 yards.

Modified may well be the single most useful all-around choke of them all. Obviously, those crafty trap shooters were on to something.

Shotgunning Implications

For the average shotgunner, all of this information is interesting, but the question is, how can you put it to use?

It is safe to say that Gil and Vicki's tests show that the old-time shotgun makers knew a thing or two. The two classic combinations—IC/M and M/F—are very hard to beat for the average game shooter facing a wide variety of situations, and in three cases out of four, IC/M is probably the best choice.

What amazed me was that at 25 yards Modified has just as good a

Gil demonstrates that at 40 yards—the generally accepted optimum shotgun range—Mod. delivers a better killing pattern than IC, which is already deteriorating badly.

killing pattern as IC, and at 40 yards a Modified outer killing pattern is considerably better than IC, which is already deteriorating badly.

Vicki Ash and the author with the Mod. pattern. Based on the Ashes' tests, Modified may be the most useful overall choke.

For practical application of this combination on birds, measure 30 yards and learn to recognize it at a glance. That is both the optimum distance for IC and its maximum, for beyond that it fades rapidly. At 35 yards, Modified takes over, delivering a larger killing pattern than IC, so it is more useful from 30 to 50 yards—the outer limit for this combination.

With M/F, it is less clear cut. However, Modified becomes the more useful of the two by a substantial margin, delivering a smallish (24-inch) but consistent killing pattern from about 35 to 50 yards. Full is at its best for a brief moment at 45 yards. Because birds are rarely at one specific distance for more than a split second, it is obvious that Modified becomes the dependable workhorse choke of this combination.

So if you are a shotgunner with one single-barrel gun, with a fixed choke, who wants to hunt a little of everything in every season under all conditions, what choke should you choose? Modified would be the best choice, followed by IC.

For a double gun, IC/M would probably be the best combination 75 percent of the time. The key, though, would be to learn exactly what 30 yards looks like and then stick rigorously to shooting the open barrel in close and reverting to Mod. at anything beyond 30 yards. It is a shocking revelation that Mod. has a larger killing pattern at 35 yards than does IC, but it's a fact—a fact that can be put to very effective use.

Gil Ash, standing and looking at his three-dimensional display of choke patterns, told me that he has yet to set up the display without seeing something, some nuance, that he has not noticed before. I feel the same way writing about it. This only scratches the surface of the lessons that are waiting for any shotgunner willing to take the time and do a little non-shooting study to improve his actual-shooting performance.

The great thing about shotgunning: You never stop learning.